Th

Gen. Thos. J. Jackson "Stonewall"

For the Young (Fourth Reader Grade), in Easy Words

Mary L. Williamson

Alpha Editions

This edition published in 2022

ISBN : 9789356904156

Design and Setting By
Alpha Editions
www.alphaedis.com
Email - info@alphaedis.com

Contents

PREFACE.

Continuing the argument set forth in the "Life of Gen. Lee for Children," that we can advance primary education and impress lessons of morality upon children in no better way than to place before them the careers of our great men, I now give, in simple words, the "Life of Gen. Thos. J. Jackson."

In this brief sketch of our great Southern hero, I have endeavored to portray, amid the blaze of his matchless military genius, the unchanging rectitude of his conduct, the stern will-power by which he conquered all difficulties, his firm belief in an overruling Providence, and his entire submission to the Divine Will. These traits of character were the corner-stones upon which he reared the edifice of his greatness, and upon which the young people of our day will do well to build.

Teachers may introduce this book as a supplementary reader into the fourth grade, as I have been careful to employ as few words as possible outside of the vocabulary of that grade.

In preparing this work, I used chiefly as reference and authority the Life of Lieut.-Gen. Thomas J. Jackson, by Prof. R. L. Dabney, D. D., who was, for a time, Jackson's chief of staff, and who had personal knowledge of his character and military exploits.

Acknowledgment is due Col. James H. Morrison for valuable assistance rendered, and to Mrs. Thomas J. Jackson, of Charlotte, N. C., and Mr. M. Miley, of Lexington, Va., for furnishing valuable illustrative matter.

I am also indebted to the kindness of Messrs. Paxton and Henkel, the editors, respectively, of the *Rockbridge County News* and the *Shenandoah Valley*, for files of their reliable journals, containing accounts of the more recent events recorded in the last chapter.

MARY LYNN WILLIAMSON.

NEW MARKET, VA.

Stonewall Jackson's Way.

DES RIVIERES.

Come! stack arms, men; pile on the rails,
Stir up the camp-fires bright;
No matter if the canteen fails,
We'll make a roaring night.
Here Shenandoah brawls along,
There lofty Blue Ridge echoes strong
To swell the brigade's rousing song
Of "Stonewall Jackson's Way."

We see him now—the old slouched hat
Cocked o'er his eye askew;
The shrewd, dry smile, the speech so pat,
So calm, so blunt, so true.
The "Blue Light Elder" knows them well:
Says he, "That's Banks—he's fond of shell;
Lord save his soul! we'll give him—" Well,
That's Stonewall Jackson's Way.

Silence! ground arms! kneel all! caps off!
"Old Blue Light's" going to pray;
Strangle the fool who dares to scoff!
Attention! it's his way:
Appealing from his native sod,
In forma pauperis to God—
"Lay bare thine arm, stretch forth thy rod;
Amen!" That's Stonewall Jackson's Way.

He's in the saddle now. Fall in!
Steady! the whole brigade!
Hill's at the ford, cut off! We'll win
His way out ball and blade.
What matter if our shoes are worn?
What matter if our feet are torn?
Quick step! we're with him e'er the morn!
That's Stonewall Jackson's Way.

The sun's bright glances rout the mists
Of morning—and, by George!
There's Longstreet struggling in the lists,
Hemmed in an ugly gorge.
Pope and his columns whipped before.—
"Bay'nets and grape!" hear Stonewall roar;
"Charge, Stuart! pay off Ashby's score!"
Is "Stonewall Jackson's Way."

CHAPTER I.
An Orphan Boy.

Thomas Jonathan Jackson was born January 21, 1824, at Clarksburg, West Virginia, which state was then a part of old Virginia. He sprang from Scotch-Irish stock. His great-grandfather, John Jackson, was born in Ireland, but his parents moved to the city of London when John was only two years old. John Jackson grew up to be a great trader. In 1748 he came to the New World to make his fortune, and landed in the State of Maryland. Not long after, he married Elizabeth Cummins, a young woman who was noted for her good looks, fine mind, and great height.

House in which Jackson was Born, Clarksburg, Va.

John Jackson with his wife soon moved West, and at last took up lands in what is now known as Upshur county, West Virginia. As land was then cheap, he soon owned a large tract of country, and was a rich man for those times. He was greatly aided by his brave wife, Elizabeth. In those days the Indians still made war upon the whites, who would flee for safety into the forts or strongholds. It is said that in more than one of those Indian raids Elizabeth Jackson aided in driving off the foe.

Father of "Stonewall" Jackson.

When the great Revolutionary war came on, John Jackson and several of his sons marched to the war; and at its close came back safe to their Virginia home. In these lovely and fertile valleys, John Jackson and his wife Elizabeth passed long and active lives. The husband lived to be eighty-six years old, while his wife lived to the great age of one hundred and five years. Her strength of body and mind fitted her to rear a race of mighty men.

Thomas Jonathan was the great-grandson of these good people. His father, Jonathan Jackson, was a lawyer. He is said to have been a man of good mind and kind heart. Thomas's mother was Julia Neale, the daughter of a merchant in the then village of Parkersburg, on the Ohio river. Mrs. Jackson was good and beautiful. Thomas had one brother, Warren, and two sisters, Elizabeth and Laura. Not long after the birth of the baby Laura, Elizabeth was taken sick with fever and died. Her father, worn out with nursing, was also taken ill; and two weeks after her death he was laid in a grave by her side.

After his death it was found that he had left no property for his widow and babes. They were now without a home, and the Masonic Order gave the widow a house of one room. Here she sewed, and taught school, caring as well as she could for her little fatherless children.

In the year 1830 she married Mr. Woodson, a lawyer, who was pleased with her youth and beauty. Her children—Warren, Thomas, and Laura—were now claimed by their father's family, who did not like the second marriage of the mother.

As her new husband was not a rich man, she was at last forced to give them up. Little Jonathan, then only seven years old, was placed behind good, old "Uncle Robinson," the last of his father's slaves, and sent away to his aunt, Mrs. Brake, who lived about four miles from Clarksburg.

After being one year at his aunt's he was sent for to see his mother die. Death for her had no sting; and Thomas, long years after, said that her dying words and prayers had never been erased from his heart. She was laid to rest not far from the famous Hawk's Nest, on New river, West Virginia.

Jonathan was then a pretty child, with rosy cheeks, wavy brown hair, and deep-blue eyes. It is said of him that, as a child, he was strangely quiet and manly. The sadness of his young life made him grave and thoughtful beyond his years. When he was but eight years old he went one day to the home of his father's cousin, Judge John G. Jackson, in Clarksburg.

While eating his dinner, he said to Mrs. Jackson in a quiet way, "Uncle and I don't agree. I have quit him and shall not go back any more." His kind cousin tried to show him that he was in fault and that he should go back to his Uncle Brake. He only shook his head and said more firmly than ever, "No, uncle and I don't agree. I have quit him and shall not go back any more." It seems that his uncle had tried to govern him by force rather than through his sense of right and wrong. So, this strange child calmly made up his mind not to stay where there would be constant warfare.

From Judge Jackson's he went that evening to the home of another cousin, who also tried to persuade him to return to his Uncle Brake. But Jonathan only said, "I have quit there. I shall not go back there any more." The next morning he set out alone and on foot, and went eighteen miles to the home of his uncle, Cummins Jackson, the half-brother of his father.

There he found his brother Warren, and soon felt quite at home with his kind uncle and aunts. His Uncle Cummins was a bachelor, who owned a fine farm and mills, and was one of the largest slave-owners in Lewis county.

He was quite fond of his little nephew, and took pains to teach him all the arts of country life. He treated him more as an equal than as a child, for he saw at once the noble nature with which he had to deal. He also sent Thomas and Warren to the nearest county school, but Warren, now a bold lad of fourteen years, did not like such restraint. He at last induced Thomas to go with him from their uncle's home to seek their fortunes in the great West.

After stopping for a time at the home of their uncle on the Ohio river, they went down that river, and for some months were not heard from.

In the fall of that year, they returned to their kind friends, ragged, and ill with chills and fever.

Their story was that they made a raft and floated down to one of the lonely islands in the Mississippi river near the Kentucky shore, where they cut wood for steamboats on the river. Here they spent the summer alone, with little food, in the midst of a dense forest surrounded by the turbid, rushing waters of the great Mississippi.

At last, illness forced them to seek their way homeward; and Thomas boldly said that he was going back to his good Uncle Cummins. Warren stopped at the home of his Uncle Brake, but disease had laid so firm a hold upon him that, after lingering a few years, he died, aged about nineteen.

Warren and Thomas on the Ohio river.

Thomas and Laura were now all that were left of the little family. They lived together for several months at their Uncle Cummins's, and it is told of

Thomas that he was very fond of his little sister. Across the brook from the house was a large grove of sugar-maple trees where they would go to play "making sugar." It was a great pleasure to Thomas to build bridges for his little sister to walk on in crossing the stream, and many were the delights of the cool and fragrant forests. But in a short time Laura was sent to live with her mother's friends in Wood county, and Thomas was left alone. Though they could not live together, Thomas always cherished the warmest love for his sister, and the very first money he ever earned was spent in buying a silk dress for her.

Thomas now went to school to Mr. Robert P. Ray. He showed no aptness for any study except arithmetic. When called upon to recite a lesson, he would flatly say that he did not understand it and, therefore, was not ready; nor would he go to the next lesson until he had learned the first perfectly. Thus, he was always behind his class. He was never surly at school, but was always ready for a merry romp or play. When there were games of "bat and ball" or "prisoner's base," he was sure to be chosen captain of one side, and that side generally won.

As long as he was treated fairly by his playmates, he was gentle and yielding; but, if he thought himself wronged, he did not hesitate to fight it out. It is said that he would never admit that he had been beaten in a fray, and was always ready to renew the contest when his foe assailed him again.

In the summer, Thomas worked on the farm and became of use to his uncle in many ways. One of his most frequent tasks was to haul great logs of oak and pine from the wood to the saw-mill. He, thus, became a famous driver of oxen, and was known throughout the country-side as a young man of great strength and courage.

So his life was passed, from nine to sixteen, between the school and the farm. He was then like his father, of low stature, but he afterwards grew tall like the men of his mother's race.

About this time, he was made constable of one-half of Lewis county. We see him now with his bag of bills and account books going up and down the hills of Lewis county. In this work he had to be firm and exact, for it was now his task to collect money due for debts.

This story is told of his nerve and skill in doing this unpleasant duty. A man who owed a debt of ten dollars promised to pay it at a given time. The day came and the man failed to keep his word. Young Jackson paid the money out of his own purse, and then watched for the man who would not pay his debt. The very next morning the man came riding up the street on a good horse. Jackson at once taxed him with not keeping his word, and was going to take the horse for the debt, when the latter resisted, and a fierce fight took place in the street. In the midst of the fray the man mounted his horse and was riding off.

Jackson, however, sprang forward and seized the bridle. Seeing that he could get the man off the horse in no other way, he led it to the low door of a stable near by. The man cuffed him right and left, but Jackson clung to the bridle, and pulled the horse into the stable. The man was thus forced to slide off to keep from being knocked off; and Jackson got the horse.

Though this life in the open air was good for the health of our hero, it did not benefit his morals. He was kept much from home, and was thrown with the worst class of people in the county.

His aunts had now married, and his Uncle Cummins was keeping "bachelor's hall." He also kept race horses, and none save Thomas could ride for him if a contest was close.

It was said through all that country that if a horse could win, he would do so if young Tom Jackson rode him in the race.

It is sad to think of this young man thrown upon the world without mother or sister or any human influence, save his own will, to keep him in the right way. But in this wild, rough life the great wish of his heart was to reach that condition from which he had been thrust when left a poor orphan boy. And even now the great God, who has said that He will be a father to the fatherless, was opening up a way to a great and notable career.

Constable (kun'-sta-ble), an officer of the peace.

Nŏ-ta-ble, wonderful.

Ca-reer', a course.

In'-flu-ence, power not seen.

Do you remember—

The name of Thomas's father?

The place of his birth?

His early loss of father and mother?

His life at Uncle Cummins's?

The story told of him when constable?

The wish of his heart in the midst of his wild, rough life?

CHAPTER II.
A Cadet.

In 1842, the place of a cadet in the great academy at West Point became vacant. In that school or academy the young men of the United States are trained to become soldiers. Thomas at once sought and secured the place, and very soon set out on horseback to Clarksburg, where he would take the coach going to Washington.

He was clad in home-spun clothes, and his whole wardrobe was packed in a pair of saddle-bags.

When he reached Clarksburg, he found that the coach had passed by; but he rode on until he overtook it and then went on to Washington city.

He was kindly met by his friend Mr. Hays, member of Congress from his district, who took him at once to the Secretary of War. The latter was so pleased with his manly bearing and direct speech that he ordered his warrant to be made out at once.

Mr. Hays wished him to stay in Washington for a few days in order to see the sights of the city, but he was content to climb to the top of the dome of the Capitol, from which he could view the whole scene at once. He was then ready to go on to West Point for examination. His great trouble now was the thought that he might not know enough to stand that examination.

Mr. Hays wrote to his friends at the academy and asked them to be easy in examining the mountain boy, who wished so much to be a soldier; and it is said that they asked him no very hard questions.

Thomas was now eighteen years old. He had a fresh, ruddy face, and was strong and full of courage.

View of West Point from Port Putnam.

The fourth-class men at this school were called by their school-mates "plebs," and were made to sweep and scrub the barracks and to do other tasks of the same kind. The third-class men would play pranks upon the new boys, some of which were quite hard to bear. Now, when they saw this country boy in his home-spun clothes, they thought that they would have rare sport out of him. But such were his courage and good temper that they soon let him alone.

He now studied hard, for, being behind his class, he had double work to do. He once said to a friend that he studied very hard for what he learned at West Point.

Just as when he was a boy, if he did not understand the lesson of the day, he would not pass over it to the next, but would work on until he knew all about it.

It was often the case that when called to the black-board to recite, he would say that he was still at work on the last lesson. This, of course, caused him to get low marks, but he was too honest to pretend to know what he did not understand at all. His teachers judged his mind sound and strong, but not quick. What he lacked in quickness, he made up in steady work; so, at the end of the fourth year, he graduated seventeenth in his class.

During the second year at West Point, he grew, as it were, by a leap to the height of six feet; and in his cadet uniform was very fine-looking.

He was neat in his attire, and kept his gun clean and bright.

It is said that one day during this year, he found that his bright musket had been stolen, and that a foul and rusty one had been put into its place.

He told the captain of his loss, and gave him a mark by which his gun might be known. That evening it was found in the hands of a fellow-cadet who had stolen it and then told a falsehood to shield himself from punishment.

Jackson had been angry because of his musket, but now he was deeply vexed at the falsehood, and asked that the cadet should be sent away, as he was unfit to remain at the academy. The friends of the boy at last prevailed upon him to waive his right of pressing the charge, and the erring cadet was let alone. Not long after, the cadet again broke the rules of the school and was sent away in disgrace.

From this we see that Jackson had at that time a hatred of all that was low and wicked.

He now wrote, in a blank book, a number of maxims as rules for his life. They touched on morals, manners, dress, the choice of friends, and the aims of life. One of these rules every boy should keep in mind. It was this:

"You may be whatever you resolve to be."

We shall see that this was indeed the guiding star of his life. Whatever he willed to do he always did by sheer force of endeavor.

At this time it is plain that it was his purpose to place his name high up on the roll of earthly honor. Beneath his shy and modest manners, there burned the wish to be truly great. His life was not yet ruled by love of Christ, but it shows some of the highest and noblest aims.

Jackson was twenty-two years old when he left West Point, June 30, 1846. He then took the rank of second lieutenant of artillery in the United States army. The artillery is that branch of an army which fights with cannon, or big guns. At that time a war was going on between the United States and Mexico. General Scott was then going to the seat of war to take the chief command of the army of the United States: and Jackson, the young lieutenant, was sent to join him in the south of Mexico.

Ca-det' (kā-det'), a military pupil.

Warrant (wŏr'-rant), a certificate.

Max'-im (măks-im), a wise saying.

Mor'als (mŏr-als), conduct.

Waive (wāv), to give up.

Tell what you remember about—

Jackson's going to West Point.

His life at West Point.

The cadet who stole his musket.

The important maxim.

His age and rank when he left West Point.

The war which was going on at that time.

CHAPTER III.
A Major of Artillery.

On the 9th day of March, 1847, thirteen thousand five hundred troops were landed in one day from the American fleet upon the sea-shore near Vera Cruz (Vā-rä Kroos).

This fine army, with its waving flags and bright guns, presented a scene of splendor which Lieutenant Jackson never forgot.

General Scott's plan was to take the city of Vera Cruz by storm, and then march over the hills and valleys and lofty mountains to the City of Mexico.

This was a hard task, and cost many lives, as I will show you.

On the 13th of March, General Scott had placed his men all around the city of Vera Cruz and was ready for battle. On the 29th of March, after a fierce battle, the city was taken by the Americans. This was the first battle in which our hero took part, and it is said that he fought bravely.

Bird's-Eye View of City of Mexico.

From Vera Cruz, the army marched on until it came to a mountain, on the crest of which was the strong fort of Cerro Gordo (Sĕr'-rō Gôr'-dō). Here, our troops were led by Captain Robert E. Lee, of the engineers, over a rough road planned by him, to the rear of the Mexicans. The Americans being in front of the Mexicans and also behind them, the latter were soon put to flight, leaving many men and guns on the battlefield.

After this battle, Jackson was placed in the light artillery, which used small cannon and moved rapidly from place to place.

This change was just what young Jackson wished, for though more dangerous, the light artillery service gave him a better chance to win the honors for which his soul thirsted.

Santa Anna, the general of the Mexicans, now brought forward another large army and placed it on the mountain heights of Cherubus'co. Here, a fierce fight took place, and the Mexicans were again driven back.

As a reward for his brave conduct in this fight, our hero was given the brevet rank of captain of artillery. The army then marched on over the mountains to the strong castle of Chapultepec (Chä-pool'-tā-pĕk'). This castle was built upon a high hill guarding the plain which led to the City of Mexico. The level plain at the foot of the mountain was covered with crops of corn and other grain, and with groves of trees. Here and there were deep and wide ditches which the farmers had dug for drains. These ditches the artillery and horsemen could not cross; in fact, the growing crops so concealed them that the men could not see them until they had reached their brinks.

Within the castle of Chapultepec were swarms of Mexican soldiers, while around its base were cannon, so placed as to sweep every road that led up to it.

On the 13th of September the assault was made on three sides at the same time. Jackson was sent with his men and guns to the northwest side. Two regiments of infantry, or footmen, marched with him.

They pushed forward, pouring shot and shell at the foe, until they were quite close to their guns, and at so short a range that Jackson in a few moments found a number of his horses killed and his men struck down or scattered by the storm of grapeshot.

Just at this time, General Worth, seeing how closely Jackson was pressed, sent him word to fall back. Jackson, however, replied that if General Worth would send him fifty more men he would march forward and take the guns which had done such deadly work.

While the troops were coming up, it is said that Jackson lifted a gun by hand across a deep ditch, and began to fire upon the Mexicans with the help of only one man, the rest of his command being either killed, wounded, or hidden in the ditch.

Jackson moving cannon across a ditch.

Soon another cannon was moved across the ditch, and in a few moments the foe was driven back by the rapid firing of these two guns.

By this time, the men storming the castle on the other two sides had fought their way in, and the Mexicans began to fall back upon the City of Mexico.

Orders had been given that when this move took place, the artillery must move forward rapidly and scatter the ranks of the foe. In an instant Jackson's guns were thundering after the Mexicans, fleeing through the gates into the city.

The next morning, September 14th, the gates were forced and the Americans marched into the city of Mexico.

For his brave conduct in the battle of Chapultepec, Jackson was raised to the rank of major.

In after years, when he was modestly telling of this battle, a young man cried out, "Major, why did you not run when so many of your men and horses were killed?" He replied, with a quiet smile, "I was not ordered to do so. If I had been *ordered* to run I should have done so."

Once, when asked by a friend if he felt no fear when so many were falling around him, he said that he felt only a great desire to perform some brave deed that would win for him lasting fame. At that time, his thoughts were chiefly fixed upon the faithful performance of his duty, and gaining honor and distinction thereby.

In the beautiful City of Mexico, the American army now rested from warfare. Some months passed before Jackson's command was ordered home. His duties being light, he began the study of the Spanish language, and was soon able to speak it well. He greatly enjoyed the fine climate of Mexico, and admired the beauty and grace of her women.

For the first time in his life, he began to think of religion and to study the Bible in search of the truth.

On May 26th, 1848, a treaty of peace was made between the United States and Mexico, and the war being over, the American troops were sent home.

Major Jackson's command was sent to Fort Hamilton, about seven miles from the city of New York. While there, he was baptized and admitted to his first communion in the Episcopal Church.

After he had been at Fort Hamilton two years, Major Jackson was sent to Fort Meade, near Tampa Bay, on the west coast of Florida. While at this place, on the 28th of March, 1851, he was elected professor of natural and experimental philosophy and artillery tactics in the Military Institute at Lexington, Virginia.

Bre-vět', a commission which gives an officer a rank above his pay.

As-sault', an attack, a violent onset.

Clī'mate, the prevailing state with regard to heat and cold, &c.

What do you remember about—

The landing of troops at Vera Cruz?

The assault upon the castle of Chapultepec?

The taking of the City of Mexico by the Americans?

The new rank of Jackson?

His life in the City of Mexico?

What he once said about running?

What happened at Fort Hamilton?

The position which he accepted March 27th, 1851?

CHAPTER IV.
A Professor.

In writing of Major Jackson as a professor, it seems highly appropriate to mention the circumstances leading to his appointment to that position.

Entrance to the Virginia Military Institute Grounds.

Reared in adverse circumstances, which prevented him in early youth from receiving the benefits of a good common-school education, by his own efforts, mainly, he fitted himself to enter the United States Military Academy at West Point. His first year's course would have discouraged him in prosecuting his studies had he not been conscious that there was that within, which, if properly nurtured, would lead to ultimate success. In his second year, he raised his general standing from 51 to 30; in the third, from 30 to 20, and in the fourth, his graduating year, from 20 to 17. His upward progress attracted attention, and one of his associates remarked: "Had Jackson remained at West Point upon a course of four years' longer study, he would have reached the head of his class."

His advancement in the Mexican war, rising rapidly from brevet second lieutenant of artillery to brevet major, was no less marked than that at the academy, and his gallant and meritorious services had been heralded to the world through the official reports of his superiors.

General Francis H. Smith, superintendent of the Virginia Military Institute, in "Institute Memorial," writes:

"It is not surprising that, when the Board of Visitors of the Virginia Military Institute were looking about for a suitable person to fill the chair of Natural and Experimental Philosophy and Artillery, the associates of this young and brave major of artillery should have pointed him out as worthy to receive so distinguished an honor. Other names had been submitted to the Board of Visitors by the Faculty of West Point, all of men distinguished for high scholarship and for gallant services in Mexico. McClellan, Reno, Rosecrans, afterward generals in the Northern army, and G. W. Smith, who afterward became a general in the Confederate army, were thus named. But the peculiar fitness of young Jackson, the high testimonials to his personal character, and his nativity as a Virginian, satisfied the Board that they might safely select him for the vacant chair without seeking candidates from other States. He was, therefore, unanimously elected to the professorship on the 28th of March, 1851, and entered upon the duties of his chair on the 1st of September following.

"The professorial career of Major Jackson was marked by great faithfulness, and by an unobtrusive, yet earnest spirit. With high mental endowments, *teaching* was a new profession to him, and demanded, in the important department of instruction assigned to him, an amount of labor which, from the state of his health, and especially from the weakness of his eyes, he rendered at great sacrifice.

"Conscientious fidelity to duty marked every step of his life here, and when called to active duty in the field he had made considerable progress in the preparation of an elementary work on optics, which he proposed to publish for the benefit of his classes.

Virginia Military Institute Barracks (fore-shortened)

"Strict, and at times stern, in his discipline, though ever polite and kind, he was not always a popular professor; but no professor ever possessed to a higher degree the confidence and respect of the cadets for his unbending integrity and fearlessness in the discharge of his duty. If he was exact in his demands upon them, they knew he was no less so in his own respect for and submission to authority; and, thus, it became a proverb among them, that it was useless to write an excuse for a report made by Major Jackson. His great principle of government was, that *a general rule should not be violated for any particular good*; and his animating rule of action was, that *a man could always accomplish what he willed to perform.*

"Punctual to a minute, I have known him to walk in front of the superintendent's quarters in a hard rain, because the hour had not quite arrived when it was his duty to present his weekly class reports.

"For ten years, he prosecuted his unwearied labors as a professor, making during this period, in no questionable form, such an impress upon those who from time to time were under his command, that, when the war broke out, the spontaneous sentiment of all cadets and graduates was, *to serve under him as their leader.*"

An incident is related by General Smith in the same work, which shows clearly how Jackson was looked upon in the community in which he resided:

"He left the Virginia Military Institute on the 21st of April, 1861, in command of the corps of cadets, and reported for duty at Camp Lee, Richmond. Dangers were thickening rapidly around the State. Invasion by overwhelming numbers seemed imminent. Norfolk, Richmond, Alexandria, and Harper's Ferry were threatened. Officers were needed to command at these points. The Governor of Virginia nominated Major Jackson as a colonel of volunteers. His nomination was immediately and unanimously confirmed by the Council of State, and sent to the Convention then in session. Some prejudice existed in that body from the supposed influence of the Virginia Military Institute in these appointments, and the question was asked by various members, 'Who is this Thomas J. Jackson'? A member of the Convention from the county of Rockbridge, Hon. S. McDowell Moore, replied: 'I can tell you who he is. *If you put Jackson in command at Norfolk, he will never leave it alive unless you order him to do so.*' Such was the impress made upon his neighbors and friends in his quiet life as a professor at the Military Institute."

In accepting the position of professor, he was again stepping higher. In active warfare an officer may advance rapidly, but in times of peace he lives quietly at a military post and simply rusts out. Ill-health, brought on mainly by exposure in the Mexican War, caused Major Jackson to resign his commission in the army; but in all probability, had this not been the case he would have abandoned army life, because he felt that by close study and application, he could reach a much higher degree of mental excellence than he had attained; and the position of professor would enable him to do this, for he knew that the best way to learn was to teach.

In consequence of the weakness of his eyes, his great will-power had now to be exerted to the utmost, because he could not use his eyes at night. In order to do himself and his classes justice, each morning after class hours, he would carefully read over the lessons for the next day, and, at night after his simple supper, he would quietly sit with his face to the wall and go over in his mind the lessons read that day. In this way he made them his own, and was prepared to teach the next day. This training was of great use to him in his after life as a soldier. The power of his mind was such that while riding, in later years, at the head of his army, he could study the movements of the foe, and plan his own with as much care and skill as in the quiet of his study at home.

The statement made by General Smith respecting the desire of the cadets to serve under Major Jackson in the war shows how popular he was, and this estimate of his powers could have been produced only by their knowledge of his great worth.

"Old Jack" was the name given to the Major by the cadets, but it was never used derisively. Pranks were played in Major Jackson's section room by the cadets, but more for their own amusement than for any other purpose. They well knew the consequences if caught, but were willing to run the risk for the sake of fun.

Cadet Abe Fulkerson once wore a collar made out of three fourths of a yard of linen, (for no other purpose than to produce a laugh) and it made even "Old Jack" laugh—that is, smile, which he would not have done if the size, shape, or color of collars had been fixed by the Institute regulations.

Cadet Davidson Penn, with an uncommonly solemn face and apparently in good faith, once asked Major Jackson, "Major, can a cannon be so bent as to make it shoot around a corner?" The Major showed not the slightest sign of impatience or of merriment, but after a moment of apparently sober thought, replied, "Mr. Penn, I reckon hardly."

It has been said that Major Jackson never smiled or laughed. It has just been shown that he smiled *once*, and there is no doubt but that if he could have been seen when he read the excuse mentioned below, not only would another smile have been seen, but a good, hearty laugh heard. At artillery drill one evening Major Jackson had given the command, "Limbers and caissons pass your pieces, trot, march!" Cadet Hambrick failed to *trot* at command and was reported. The next day the following excuse was handed in: Report, "Cadet Hambrick not trotting at artillery drill." Excuse, "I am a natural pacer." These three incidents are recounted by Dr. J. C. Hiden, of Richmond, Virginia.

Professor Jackson's Class-room, Virginia Military Institute.

Cadet Thos. B. Amiss, who was afterwards surgeon of one of Jackson's Georgian regiments, tried a prank for the double purpose of evading a recitation and creating a laugh. He was squad-marcher of his section, and after calling the roll and making his report to the officer of the day, he turned the section over to the next man on the roll, took his place in ranks, and cautioned the new squad-marcher not to report him absent. While the squad marcher was making his report to Major Jackson whose eyes seemed always riveted to his class-book when this was being done, Amiss noiselessly climbed to the top of a column that stood nearly in the center of the room. Having received the report, Major Jackson commenced to call the names of those whom he wished to recite at the board, commencing with Amiss; not hearing Amiss respond, he asked, "Mr. Amiss absent?" The squad-marcher replied, "No, sir." The Major looked steadily along the line of faces, seemed perplexed and cast his eyes upwards, when he spied the delinquent at the top of the column. The Major, for a moment, gazed at the clinging figure and said, "You stay there," and Amiss had to remain where he was until the recitation was over. He was reported, court-martialed, received the maximum number of demerits, and had a large number of extra tours of guard duty assigned him, during the walking of which in the lone hours of the night, he had ample time to repent of his folly.

When the class that graduated in 1860 commenced its recitations under Major Jackson, a sudden end was made to all kinds of merriment in his class-room. A member of the class, who is now a member of Congress from Virginia, concealed a small music-box under his coatee and carried it into the class-room. After the recitation had commenced he touched a spring and the room was filled with sweet, muffled strains of music. Major Jackson did not hear, or if he did, took no notice of it. The cadet, finding that his music was not duly appreciated, commenced to bark, in very low tones, like a puppy, and this meeting with the same fate as the music he became emboldened and barked louder. Major Jackson, without changing his countenance, turning his head, or raising his voice above an ordinary tone, said, "Mr. C., when you march the section in again, please leave that puppy outside." The laugh was on the young cadet, and the result stated followed.

The following incident illustrates clearly how regardless Major Jackson was of public opinion or personal feeling when in conflict with duty. A young cadet was dismissed through a circumstance that occurred in Major Jackson's class-room, and he became so enraged that he challenged the Major to fight a duel, and sent him word that if he would not fight he would kill him on sight. Major Jackson, actuated solely by conscientious motives, took the necessary precautions to prevent a conflict, and informed the young man, through his friends, that if he were attacked he would defend himself. The attack was not made, notwithstanding the fact that the Major passed back and forth as usual. This cadet, during the Civil War, learned to know Major Jackson better, was under his command, and before the close of the war commanded the "Stonewall Brigade," which was rendered so famous by Jackson; and in later years, when asked his opinion of this great man, said that he was the only man ever born who had never been whipped.

Major Jackson seemed to enjoy the duty of drilling the artillery battery more than any other duty he had to perform, and it was natural that he should, for he had won fame as an artillery officer in the Mexican War.

Where Major Jackson trained artillerymen (Virginia Military Institute Parade-Grounds).

Near the close of every session of the Institute, Major Jackson was required to drill the battery before the Board of Visitors; and in order to make it more interesting to the public, always present in large crowds, blank cartridges were fired, and the drill had really the semblance of a battery in actual battle. An impressive scene was witnessed at this drill in 1860. It commenced at 5 P. M. Major Jackson had put the battery through its various evolutions, and as the time approached for the firing to commence, seemed more and more interested in his work. His old professor of engineering at West Point, Dennis Mahan, and the commandant of cadets of that institution, Colonel Hardee, witnessed the drill. Ever since the commencement of the evolutions, a dark cloud had been gathering in the west and the rumbling of thunder could be heard. The firing commenced and all was excitement. Closer and closer came the cloud, and the artillery of heaven seemed replying to the discharges of the battery. Major Jackson had been slowly retreating before the imaginary foe, firing by half battery. The cloud came nearer and nearer, unheeded by Jackson. Suddenly his voice rang clear and sharp, "Fire advancing by half battery"—the foe were retreating—"right-half battery advance, commence firing!" New positions were rapidly taken, and the firing was at its height. Then the storm broke in all its fury. Up to that time the Major had seemed oblivious to all save the drill. The bursting storm brought him to himself and he dismissed the battery, which at once went to shelter. Major Jackson remained where he was, folded his arms and stood like a statue in the driving storm. An umbrella was sent him from a house close by with an invitation to come to cover. He replied, "No, thank you;" and there he stood until the storm was over, doubtless thinking of the hard-fought fields of Mexico and the havoc he had there wrought.

In November, 1851, Major Jackson connected himself with the Presbyterian church at Lexington, then in charge of the Rev. Dr. W. S. White. It now seemed his chief desire to do good. He was made a deacon and given a class of young men in the Sunday school. Some of them still live and remember how faithfully he taught them. He also gathered together the African slaves of the town every Sabbath evening for the purpose of teaching them the truths of the Bible. He soon had a school of eighty or a hundred pupils and twelve teachers. This school he kept up from 1855 to 1861, when he left Lexington to enter the army; and until his death it was always a great pleasure to him to hear of his black Sunday school.

Duty became now more than ever the rule of his life—duty to God and duty to man. So great was his regard for the Sabbath that he would not even read a letter, or mail one which he knew would be carried on that day.

The Rev. R. L. Dabney tells us that one Sabbath, when a dear friend, who knew that the Major had received a letter from his lady-love late on Saturday night, asked, as they were walking to church, "Major, surely you have read your letter?" "Certainly not," said he. "What obstinacy!" exclaimed his friend. "Do you not think that your desire to know its contents will distract your mind from divine worship far more than if you had done with reading it?" "No," answered he, quietly, "I shall make the most faithful effort I can to control my thoughts, and as I do this from a sense of duty, I shall expect the divine blessing upon it."

When a single man, he made it a rule to accept, if possible, all invitations, saying that when a friend had taken the trouble to invite him it was his duty to attend.

Major Gittings, once a cadet, and a relative of Major Jackson, says: "Speaking from a social standpoint, no man ever had a more delicate regard for the feelings of others than he, and nothing would embarrass him more than any *contretemps* that might occur to cause pain or distress of mind to others. Hence, he was truly a polite man, and while his manner was often constrained, and even awkward, yet he would usually make a favorable impression, through his desire to please."

When Major Jackson first came to Lexington he was in ill-health, and many things he did were looked upon as odd, which were really not so. He had been at a famous water-cure hospital in the North, and had been ordered to live on stale bread and buttermilk and to wear a wet shirt next to his body. He was also advised to go to bed at 9 o'clock. If that hour found him at a party or lecture, or any other place, in order to obey his physician, he would leave.

Major Jackson's Home in Lexington.

The dyspepsia with which he suffered often caused drowsiness, and he would sometimes go to sleep while talking to a friend or while sitting in his pew at church.

General Hill says of him: "I have seen his head bowed down to his very knees during a good part of the sermon. He always heard the text of our good pastor, the Rev. Dr. White, and the first part of the sermon, but after that all was lost." Before leaving Lexington, he seemed to have gained complete control over his muscles, even while asleep, for no one, in the few years preceding his departure, ever saw "his head and his knees in contact," but it was a common thing to see him sound asleep while sitting perfectly upright.

Before marriage, Major Jackson had his room in barracks, but took his meals at a hotel in Lexington, and it has been said by some that his eccentricities caused much comment; more than that, he was laughed at and insulted by rude, coarse persons. This could hardly have been true, for an insult offered to "Old Jack" would certainly have been found out in some way, and if not resented personally, it would have been by the cadets to a man. One who lived in Lexington during four years of Major Jackson's residence there, and more than a quarter of a century after the war, never heard of these insults, and, surely, had they ever been given they would have been talked of, for Jackson's name was on every tongue, and the incidents of his life, from boyhood to death, were almost a constant subject of conversation.

Though Major Jackson was very modest, no man ever relied more fully upon himself. Mentioning one day to a friend that he was going to begin the study of Latin, he received the reply that one who had not studied the forms of that language in youth could never become master of it in later years. To this Jackson replied, "No; if I attempt it, I shall become master of the language. *I can do what I will to do.*"

This stern will-power came to the aid of his ambition many times. He found it difficult to speak in public, and in order to acquire the art, he joined a literary club called the "Franklin Society." He was always at the meetings, and spoke in his turn; but, at first, his efforts were painful both to himself and to his hearers. His health was poor, his nerves were unstrung, and sometimes he was so confused that he would break down in the middle of a sentence for want of the right word. When this happened, he would quietly sit down, and when his turn in the debate came again would rise and make another attempt. Thus, before the close of the debate, he would succeed in telling what was in his mind. By thus trying time after time, he became a good speaker.

Soon after joining the Presbyterian church, good Dr. White, his pastor, called upon him to pray in public. He prayed in such a halting way that Dr. White told him that he would never again ask him to perform so hard a task. Major Jackson replied that it was a cross to him to pray in public, but that he had made up his mind to bear it, and did not wish to be excused. So he kept on trying, and soon became a leader in prayer.

General Hill, speaking of this incident, says: "I think his conduct in this case was due to his determination to conquer every weakness of his nature. He once told me that when he was a small boy, being sick, a mustard plaster was placed upon his chest, and his guardian mounted him upon a horse to go to a neighbor's house, so that his mind might be diverted and the plaster kept on. He said that the pain was so dreadful that he fainted soon after getting off his horse. I asked him if he had kept it on in order to obey his guardian. He answered, 'No, it was owing to a feeling that I have had from childhood not to yield to trials and difficulties.'"

The same close friend also writes: "Dr. Dabney thinks that he was timid, and that nothing but his iron will made him brave. I think this is a mistake. The muscles of his face would twitch when a battle was about to open, and his hand would tremble so that he could hardly write. His men would see the working of his face and would say, 'Old Jack is making faces at the

Yankees.' But all this only showed weak nerves. I think he loved danger for its own sake."

Like St. Paul, "he kept his body under," and would not let any appetite control him or any weakness overcome him. He used neither coffee, tobacco, nor spirits, and he would go all winter without cloak or overcoat in the mountains of Virginia, giving as a reason that he "did not wish to give way to cold."

For a like reason, he never drank spirits of any kind. It is told of him that once during the Civil War, when he was too near the outposts of the foe to have fire, and being greatly chilled, he was advised by his surgeon to take a drink of brandy. He at length agreed to take some, but made such a wry face in swallowing it that some one asked him if it choked him. "No," he replied, "I like it. That is the reason I never use it." Another time, being asked to take a drink of brandy, he said, "No, I thank you; I am more afraid of it than all the Federal bullets."

The immortal Jackson afraid of strong drink! What a lesson to people who have not the courage to say "No," when tempted to do wrong!

In the midst of this busy life as professor, Major Jackson was married, on August 4th, 1853, to Miss Eleanor Junkin, the daughter of the president of Washington College, Lexington, Virginia. This lovely lady lived only fourteen months after her marriage. Major Jackson's grief at her death was so great as to alarm his friends. His health, never good, suffered seriously, and his friends induced him in the summer of 1856 to take a trip to Europe, hoping that "the spell might be broken which bound him to sadness."

His European trip benefited him very materially in health and spirits, and on his return he, with great zeal, resumed his labors in his classes at both the Military Institute and the Sunday School.

He had started on his return trip in ample time to reach the Institute at its opening, September 1st, which he had promised to do; but storms had prevented this and he was behind time.

A lady friend, knowing what a slave he was to his word, asked him if he had not been miserable at the delay. The answer was characteristic of the man. He had done his part, Providence had intervened, and he had not worried in the least. No man ever trusted Providence more implicitly than Jackson, and when he went to God in prayer he knew that his feet would be guided in the right way.

Dr. Dabney tells us that one day, when a friend said that he could not understand how one could "pray without ceasing," Jackson replied that he had, for some time, been in the habit of praying all through the day. "When we take our meals," said he, "there is grace, and when I take a draught of water, I always pause to lift up my heart to God in thanks for the 'water of life'; and when I go to my class-room and await the coming of the cadets, that is my time to pray for them. And so with every other act of the day." Thus we see that Jackson was truly a "praying man."

His pastor, Rev. Dr. White, once said that Major Jackson was the happiest man that he had ever known. This happiness came from his faith in the saving care of God.

We are told that a friend once said to him, "Suppose you should lose your eyesight and then, too, be very ill, and have to depend on those bound to you by no tie, would not this be too much for your faith? Do you think you could be happy then?" He thought a moment and then said, "If it were the will of God to place me on a sick bed, He would enable me to lie there in peace a hundred years."

Such was the faith of this great man! As he grew older his spirit became more saintly until, when called upon to go up higher to meet his Lord, his end seemed more like a passing over than a death.

Major Jackson was married again, on July 15th, 1857, to Mary Anna Morrison, the daughter of Dr. R. H. Morrison, a Presbyterian minister, of North Carolina. This lady is now living, and has quite lately written a life of her husband, in which she gives beautiful glimpses of their home life in Lexington, and also extracts from his letters written to her during the Civil War, of which I must so soon tell you.

Shortly after his second marriage, Major Jackson bought a house and a few acres of land, and soon all of his spare time was spent in working in his garden and fields.

We are told that his little farm of rocky hill-land was soon well fenced and tilled, and that he used to say that the bread grown there by the labor of himself and slaves tasted sweeter than that which was bought.

Mrs. T. J. Jackson in 1899.

He liked to have his friends visit him, and nowhere else was he so easy and happy as with his guests at his own table.

In his home, military sternness left his brow and the law of love took its place.

This story is told of him, which shows how gentle and tender a soldier may be. "Once a friend, who was taking his little four-year-old girl on a journey without her mother, called on the way to spend the night with Major Jackson. At bed-time, when Mrs. Jackson wished to take the child to her room for the night, the father replied that his little one would give less trouble if he kept her with him. In the still watches of the night, he heard a soft step, and felt a hand laid upon his bed. It was Major Jackson, who, fearing that the little girl would toss off the covering, had come to see that all was safe."

This good and peaceful life at Lexington was short. The black cloud of war was hovering over our land and ere long the storm burst in great fury, sweeping Major Jackson away from his quiet life, his professorial duties, and his loved wife and friends, into the midst of carnage and death, and to deeds that made his fame world-wide and immortal.

Major Jackson had but one more duty to perform as a professor and officer of the Virginia Military Institute. He had been left in charge of the corps of cadets when the superintendent had been called to Richmond. Early on the morning of Sunday, April 21st, 1861, an order was received by Major Jackson from Governor John Letcher, directing him to leave with his command for Richmond at 12:30 P. M. that day. Major Jackson's arrangements were promptly made, and he sent a request to his pastor, good Dr. White, to come to the Institute and hold religious services for the young men prior to their departure. These services were held in front of the barracks. The battalion was drawn up in line of battle, Major Jackson at the head and venerable Dr. White in the front and center. All, with bowed heads, were devoutly listening to the invocations speeding heavenward. The clock in the Institute tower gave the signal for departure, and, without a moment's pause, Jackson took up the line of march and left his beloved pastor praying.

The key-note of his great success as a soldier was prompt obedience to orders and requiring the same of others.

Me-mo'ri-al, something designed to keep in remembrance a person, place, or event.

Fac'ul-ty, the body of instructors in a school.

Prof-es-so'ri-al, pertaining to a professor.

Coat-ee' (cō-tē'), a short military coat.

Con'sci-en'-tious, governed by conscience.

Ŏb'sti-na-cy, stubbornness.

Tell about—

Major Jackson's appointment as professor in the Virginia Military Institute.

His reasons for resigning his position in the army and accepting a professorship.

His life at the Institute.

His method of studying.

His Sunday school for negroes.

His strict observance of the Sabbath.

His home life.

CHAPTER V.
A Confederate Colonel.

Before going on with the life of our hero, I must tell you, in a few plain and truthful words, the causes of the Civil War which in 1861 broke out between the States.

You remember that, after the Revolutionary War, the thirteen colonies agreed to form a Union, and adopted a set of laws called the Constitution of the United States.

From the very first, however, the States did not agree; in fact, laws which suited one section did not suit the other, so that there was always some cause for a quarrel.

At last, the question of slavery seemed to give the most trouble. You have been told that African slaves were first brought to Virginia in 1619 by the Dutch, and that afterwards English and Northern traders brought others, until all of the colonies held slaves.

The cold climate of the North did not suit the negroes, who had been used to the hot sun of Africa. So, by degrees, they were sold to Southern planters.

Many influential men North and South wished to see the slaves freed. But, as the slaves increased in the South, Southern men saw that a rapid abolition of slavery would be disastrous to both whites and blacks, because the negroes were not ready for it. As slavery decreased in the North, many Northern people did not realize this. Besides, the North did not wish slave labor to compete with the free labor of the North.

The North insisted that slaves should not be brought into the new States as they came into the Union. The South demanded that a slave-holder should be free to carry his slaves from one State into another.

Many Southern people also believed that the negroes were the happiest and best cared for working people in the world, and that the North was trespassing upon their just rights.

So the quarrel went on until October, 1859, when an event happened in Virginia which greatly increased the hatred of both parties. A man named John Brown laid a plot for freeing the negroes, first in Virginia and then in the whole South.

For two years, he sent men through the South secretly to stir up the negroes and incite them to kill the whites. He bought long iron pikes for the negroes to fight with, as they did not know how to use fire-arms.

When he thought that all was ready, he entered Harper's Ferry by night, with only eighteen men, and seized the arsenal there, sending out armed men into the country to capture the principal slave-owners and to call upon the slaves to join him. This was done secretly during the night, and the next morning every white man who left his home was seized, and imprisoned in an engine-house near the arsenal. Only a few negroes came in, and they were too much scared to aid in the deadly and dastardly work.

As soon as the news of this raid spread over the country, angry men came into town from all sides, and before night John Brown and his men were shut up in the engine-house.

Harper's Ferry, Virginia.

Soon a band of marines, under the command of Colonel R. E. Lee, was sent out from Washington by the Government, and as John Brown would not surrender, the soldiers at once stormed the engine-house. Ten of John Brown's men were killed by the soldiers, and all the rest, including Brown himself, were wounded. Six of the storming party were killed and nine wounded. John Brown and seven of his men were brought to trial at Charles Town, Virginia, and being found guilty of treason, were hanged.

The cadets of the Virginia Military Institute were ordered to Charles Town to protect the officers of the law. Major Jackson commanded a section of light artillery accompanying the battalion, and was present at the death of Brown. He afterwards gave his friends a graphic account of this dreadful scene.

This event cast great gloom over the country. Many persons at the North thought that John Brown had died a martyr to the cause of slavery, while the people at the South saw that they could no longer enjoy in peace and safety the rights granted to them by the Constitution.

Major Jackson was truly Southern in feeling. He believed in the "Rights of States" and also that the South ought to take her stand and resent all efforts to coerce and crush her. He, however, dreaded war and thought it the duty of Christians throughout the land to pray for peace.

A month before South Carolina went out of the Union, Major Jackson called upon his pastor, Dr. White, and said: "It is painful to know how carelessly they speak of war. If the Government insists upon the measures now threatened, there must be war. They seem not to know what its horrors are. Let us have meetings to pray for peace." Dr. White agreed to his request, and the burden of Major Jackson's prayer was that God would preserve the land from war.

After the election of Mr. Lincoln, in November, 1860, to be President of the United States, the Southern States saw no hope of getting their rights and resolved to secede, or withdraw from the Union of the States.

South Carolina took the lead and seceded on the 20th of December, 1860. She was quickly followed by Mississippi, Alabama, Florida, Georgia, Louisiana, and Texas.

On the 9th of January, 1861, these States united and at Montgomery, in Alabama, formed a government called "The Confederate States of America," with Jefferson Davis as President.

Virginia was slow to withdraw from the Union formed by the States; but, when President Lincoln called for seventy-five thousand soldiers to invade the Southern States, she delayed no longer. On April 17th, 1861, she seceded and began to prepare for war.

"In one week," says Dabney, "the whole State was changed into a camp." The sons of Virginia rushed to arms, and soon the city of Richmond was filled with men drilling and preparing to fight.

At daybreak on Sunday morning, April 21st, 1861, an order came to Lexington from the Governor of the State (Governor Letcher) to march the cadets that day to Richmond. As the senior officers were already in Richmond, Major Jackson at once prepared to go forward with his corps.

View of the Business Portion of Richmond, Va., after the Evacuation Fire of 1865.

At eleven o'clock A. M. he went to his home to say good-bye to his wife. They retired to their own room, where he read the 5th chapter of Second Corinthians, which begins with these beautiful words: "For we know, if our earthly house of this tabernacle be dissolved, we have a building of God, an house not made with hands, eternal in the heavens."

He then knelt and prayed for themselves and for their dear country, imploring God that it might be His holy will to avert war and bloodshed. He then said good-bye to his wife and left his dear home, never more to return to it. After a few days, his wife went to live at the home of a friend—his house was closed.

Major Jackson and the cadets marched forward to Staunton, whence they went by train to Richmond, and at once went into camp on the Fair-Grounds.

From Richmond, Major Jackson wrote thus to his wife: "Colonel Lee, of the army, is here and has been made Major-General of the Virginia troops. I regard him a better officer than General Scott."

After a few days, on April 21st, Major Jackson was made colonel of the Virginia forces and ordered to take command at Harper's Ferry, a town on the Potomac river where the United States Government had had a great number of workshops and fire-arms. This important place had already been captured by Virginia troops, and it was necessary to hold it until the arms and machinery could be moved away.

Just here it may be well to give you a word-picture of our hero as he began a career which was to fill the world with his fame.

Colonel Thomas J. Jackson.

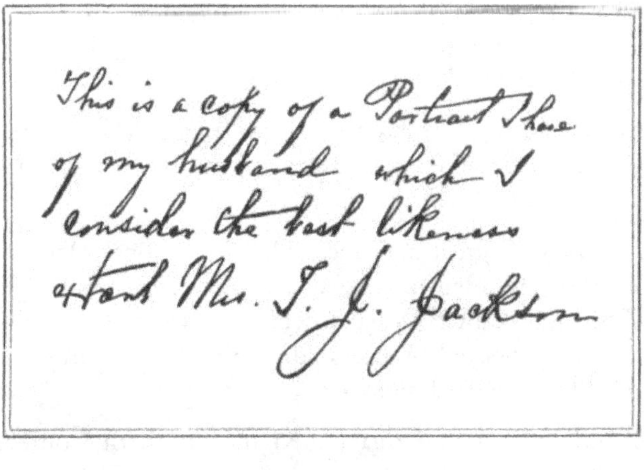

This is a copy of a Portrait I have
of my husband which I
consider the best likeness
extant Mrs. T. J. Jackson

This is a copy of a Portrait I have of my husband which I consider the best likeness extant Mrs. T. J. Jackson

Jackson was tall and very erect, with large hands and feet. His brow was fair and broad; his eyes were blue placid and clear when their owner was calm, but dark and flashing when he was aroused. His nose was Roman, his cheeks ruddy, his mouth firm, and his chin covered with a brown beard. His step was long and rapid, and if he was not a graceful rider, he was a fearless one. In battle, or as he rode along his columns, hat in hand, bowing right and left to his soldiers, whose shouts arose on high, no figure could be nobler than his. Few, even of his intimate friends, were conscious of his military genius, so he burst upon the world as a meteor darts across a star-lit sky.

On his way to Harper's Ferry, he wrote thus to his dear wife:

"WINCHESTER, April 29th, 1861.

"I expect to leave here about two P. M. to-day for Harper's Ferry. I am thankful to say that an ever-kind Providence, who causes 'all things to work together for good to them that love Him,' has given me the post which I prefer above all others. To His name be all the praise. * * * You must not expect to hear from me very often, as I shall have more work than I have ever had in the same time before; but don't be troubled about me, as an ever-kind Heavenly Father will give me all needful aid."

"This letter," says a friend, "gives a true idea of his character. He feels within himself the genius and power which make him long to have a separate command; but he also feels the need of resting upon his Heavenly Father for aid and support."

Colonel Jackson had been ordered by Major-General Lee to organize and drill the men who had gathered at Harper's Ferry and to hold the place as long as possible against the foe.

He went to work with great zeal and, aided by Colonel Maury and Major Preston, soon had the men organized into companies and regiments. As Colonel Jackson was known to have been a brave soldier in the Mexican War, he was readily obeyed by the soldiers in his little army, which soon numbered forty-five hundred men.

But on the 2nd of May, Virginia joined the Southern Confederacy and handed over all of her soldiers to that government, which bound itself in return to defend Virginia and to pay her troops.

General Joseph E. Johnston was sent on the 23rd of May by the Confederate Government to take command at Harper's Ferry and Colonel Jackson at once gave up his trust to General Johnston.

The Virginia regiments at that place—the Second, the Fourth, the Fifth, the Twenty-seventh, and a little after, the Thirty-third, with Pendleton's battery of light field-guns—were now organized into a brigade, of which Jackson was made the commander. This was the brigade which afterwards became famous as the "Stonewall Brigade," and which, we shall see, did much hard fighting, and was to the Southern army what the "Tenth Legion" was to the great Cæsar.

Gen. J. E. Johnston.

General Johnston soon found out that he could not hold Harper's Ferry against the foe which was now coming up under General Patterson. He, therefore, burnt the great railroad bridge over the Potomac river at Harper's Ferry and moved away all his guns and stores; then on Sunday, June 16th, he withdrew his little army to Bunker Hill, a place about twelve miles from the city of Winchester. There he offered battle to General Patterson, but the latter refused to fight and withdrew to the north bank of the Potomac.

On June 19th, Colonel Jackson was ordered to march northward and watch the foe, who was again crossing the river. He was also ordered to destroy the engines and cars of the Baltimore and Ohio railroad at Martinsburg.

This he did, though he writes of it in the following words: "It was a sad work; but I had my orders, and my duty was to obey."

Until July 2nd, Colonel Jackson, with his brigade, remained a little north of Martinsburg, having in his front Colonel J. E. B. Stuart with a regiment of cavalry. On that day General Patterson advanced to meet Jackson, who went forward with only one regiment, the Fifth Virginia, a few companies of cavalry, and one light field piece. A sharp skirmish ensued. At last, the foe coming up in large numbers, Jackson fell back to the main body of his troops after having taken forty-five prisoners, and killed and wounded a large number of the enemy. Jackson's loss was only two men killed and ten wounded.

In this battle, which is known as that of Haines's Farm, Colonel Jackson was, no doubt, the only man in the infantry who had ever been under fire, but they all behaved with the greatest coolness and bravery.

Jackson, in this first battle, showed such boldness, and at the same time such care for the lives of his men, that he at once gained a hold upon their esteem.

General Patterson now held Martinsburg; while General Johnston, having come up with the whole army, offered him battle each day. But Patterson had other plans, and soon moved away.

While General Johnston was at Winchester watching his movements, Colonel Jackson received this note:

"RICHMOND, July 3rd, '61.

My Dear General:

I have the pleasure of sending you a commission of Brigadier-General in the Provisional Army; and to feel that you merit it. May your advancement increase your usefulness to the State.

Very truly, R. E. LEE."

General Jackson, for so we must now call him, was much pleased at this promotion, and wrote to his wife thus:

"Through the blessing of God, I have now all that I ought to wish in the line of promotion. May His blessing rest on you is my fervent prayer."

Ar'sē-nal, a storehouse for arms and military stores.

Ma-rïnes', soldiers doing duty on a ship.

Mär'tyr, one who is put to death for the truth.

Sēn'ior (sèn-yur), one older in age or office.

Vŏl-ŭn-teer', one who enters into any service of his own free will.

Mē'teor, a shining body passing through the air.

Cæ'sar (sé-zär), a great Roman general.

Do you remember—

What happened in October 1859?

When Virginia seceded from the Union?

When Major Jackson left Lexington with the cadets?

Of what place Colonel Jackson first took command?

About Jackson's first battle?

General Robert E. Lee.

CHAPTER VI.
A Brigadier-General.

During the spring of 1861, the States of North Carolina, Tennessee, and Arkansas, also left the Union and joined the new Confederacy, the capital of which was now Richmond, Virginia.

The great object of the North was to capture Richmond. For this they raised four large armies to invade Virginia. The first was to go by way of Fortress Monroe; the second, by way of Manassas; the third was to march up the Shenandoah Valley; and the fourth was to come from the northwest.

Turn to the map of Virginia on the opposite page and find the places which I have mentioned, and you will understand the plan at once.

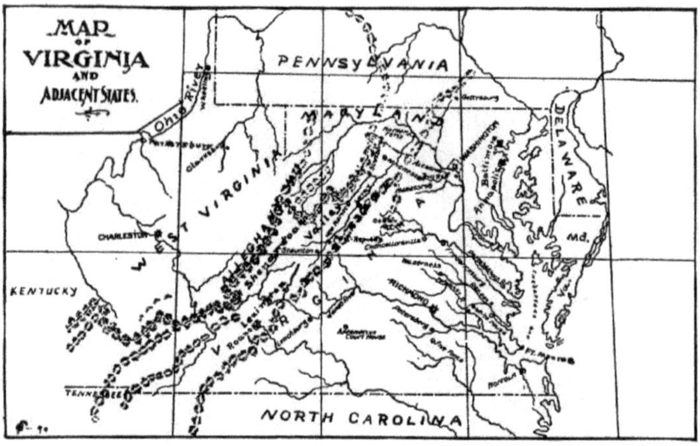

MAP OF VIRGINIA AND ADJACENT STATES.

Now, the Confederate army was much smaller than the Federal army, because the Southern States were thinly settled, while the North contained very many large cities and had the world from which to draw supplies of men as well as munitions of war.

General Beauregard.

The North also was rich, because it had the treasury of the United States, while the South was poor in both money and arms, and had the outside world closed against her.

So the Confederate leaders had to use great skill in meeting such large armies with so few men.

You remember that in the last chapter I told how General Johnston, at Winchester, with a small force was watching General Patterson. Now, just across the mountains, sixty miles southeast, at Manassas, Beauregard (bo-re-gard), another famous Southern general, was facing a large Northern army under General McDowell. This army was thirty-five thousand strong, while the Confederates had only twenty-eight thousand men. General McDowell's army was composed of the best soldiers in the Northern States, and they had splendid fire-arms, artillery, uniforms, and tents—in fact, all that money could buy to make them do good service in the field.

On the other hand, the Confederates were poorly clad and had old muskets and cannon; many of the cavalry had only the shot-guns which they had used for hunting in their boyhood days.

The North fully expected that this fine army would crush the Confederates at one blow, and, when General McDowell was a little slow in marching forward to battle, began to cry, "On to Richmond."

Large crowds of idlers, editors, reporters, members of Congress, government officials, and even ladies went from Washington to the rear of the Federal army in order to witness the defeat of the Confederates.

General Beauregard now sent word to General Johnston to leave Patterson and come across the mountains to his aid. General Johnston at once sent Colonel Stuart with his cavalry to face Patterson, and to try to keep him from finding out that Johnston had left Winchester and had gone to the help of Beauregard.

This order Stuart obeyed so well that Johnston was at Manassas, sixty miles away, before Patterson discovered the ruse.

General Johnston's army set out from Winchester on the forenoon of Thursday, July 18th. The First Virginia Brigade, led by General Jackson, headed the line of march. As they passed through the streets of Winchester, the people asked, with sad faces, if they were going to hand them over to the foe. The soldiers, for reply, said that they knew not where, or for what purpose, they were marching southeast.

But when they had marched about three miles, General Johnston called a halt, and an order was read to them explaining that they were going to Beauregard, who was then on the eve of a great battle with McDowell. The General hoped that his troops would act like men and save their country.

At these words, the men rent the air with their shouts and went forward at a double-quick, waded the Shenandoah river, which was waist deep, crossed the Blue Ridge mountains at Ashby's Gap, and some hours after night paused to rest for awhile at the village of Paris, on the eastern slope of the mountains.

Dr. Dabney tells us that here, while the men slept, Jackson himself kept watch, saying, "Let the poor fellows sleep; I will guard the camp myself." For two hours he paced up and down under the trees, or sat on the fence. At last, an hour before daybreak, he gave up his watch to a member of his staff, and rolling himself upon the grass in a fence-corner, was soon fast asleep.

"Let the poor fellows sleep; I will guard the camp myself."

At peep of day, the brigade was up and away, and, by dusk on July 19th, the whole command, dusty, hungry, and foot-sore, marched into an old pine-field near Manassas, where they spent Saturday in resting for the coming battle.

The Confederate lines stretched for eight miles along the southern bank of Bull Run, which could be forded at several places. At these fords General Beauregard had placed large bodies of men. On July 18th, before Jackson had come up, General McDowell had tried to take these fords, but his troops had been driven back.

He then made a plan to march a part of his forces around the Confederates' left wing at a certain stone bridge, and to get in their rear. Being thus between two large forces, the Confederates would be crushed or forced to surrender.

On Sunday morning, July 21st, General McDowell sent forward a portion of his troops to the stone bridge, which was guarded at that time by the gallant Colonel Evans, with only eleven hundred men. After he had fought desperately for several hours, and just as he was outflanked and sorely beset, Generals Bee and Bartow came up to his aid, and for awhile turned the tide of battle.

At last, however, the Confederates were slowly forced back by larger numbers. At this moment, General Jackson reached the spot with his brigade of two thousand six hundred men. These he quickly placed on the crest of a ridge in the edge of a pine thicket, and before them posted seventeen cannon.

Generals Bee and Bartow and Colonel Evans rallied their broken lines on the right; while on the left were a few regiments of Virginia and Carolina troops. The whole force numbered about six thousand five hundred men. The infantry of his brigade were ordered by Jackson to lie down behind the artillery to escape the fire of the enemy, who were now coming across the valley and up the hill with twenty thousand men and twenty-four cannon. Just then, Generals Johnston and Beauregard galloped to the front and cheered the men on in every part of the field.

From eleven o'clock A. M. until three o'clock P. M., the artillery shook the earth with its dreadful roar, and thousands of musket-balls whizzed through the air, black with the smoke of battle.

While the artillery fight was going on, General Jackson rode back and forth between the guns and his regiments lying prone upon the ground in the burning sun, and greatly tried by bursting shell and grape-shot. His erect form and blazing eyes brought hope and courage to them in this their first baptism of fire.

"There is Jackson, standing like a Stone Wall!"

At last General Bee, seeing his thin ranks begin to waver, said, "General, they are beating us back." "Then," said Jackson, "we will give them the bayonet." Bee, catching the spirit of Jackson, galloped back to his men, saying, "There is Jackson, standing like a stone wall! Rally behind the Virginians!" A few score of the men rallied around the gallant Bee and charged upon the foe. In a few moments the brave Bee fell dead, with his face to the foe. "From that time," says Draper, an historian of the North, "the name which Jackson had received in a baptism of fire, displaced that which he had received in a baptism of water, and he was known ever after as 'Stonewall Jackson.'"

Both of Jackson's flanks were now in danger, and he saw that the moment had come to use the bayonet. Wheeling his cannon to right and left, he gave the signal to his men to rise, and cried out to the Second regiment, "Reserve your fire until they come within fifty yards; and then fire and give them the bayonet; and when you charge, yell like furies."

His men sprang to their feet, fired one deadly volley, and then dashed down upon the foe. The latter could not stand this dreadful onset, but turned and fled. A battery which had been captured by the foe was retaken, and the centre of the enemy's line of battle pierced by Jackson's men.

For four hours, Jackson had kept the enemy at bay, but now help was near at hand. Just as the Federals had rallied and again advanced in large numbers, General Kirby Smith, with a body of men which had just come from the Valley, and Generals Early and Holmes, with reserve troops, hurried up and struck the right wing of the Federal army, while the Confederates in the centre turned against them their own guns. This onset proved too much for the Federals. They again fled; and this time, their retreat became a general rout. The men in terror cast away their guns, and leaving cannon and flags, rushed for the nearest fords of Bull Run. The Confederate cavalry pursued them, while Kemper's field battery ploughed them through and through with shells. The road to Washington was one surging mass of human beings struggling to get away from the dreadful field of death.

General Jackson's troops took no part in pursuit except to plant a battery and fire at the fleeing foe, many of whom did not stop until they were safe across the Long Bridge at Washington.

Rout of Federal Troops at Manassas.

Though the Confederates were the victors, they had lost many brave men. Generals Bee and Bartow were killed, and General Kirby Smith was badly wounded. General Jackson had been wounded in his left hand early in the action, but had taken no notice of it. Now that the battle was over, he felt the pain acutely, and went to the field-hospital, which had been placed by the side of a brook beneath the shade of some friendly willow-trees.

When he came up, his friend, Dr. McGuire, said, "General, are you much hurt?" "No," replied he; "I believe it is a trifle." "How goes the day?" asked the Doctor. "Oh!" exclaimed Jackson, "We have beaten them; we have gained a glorious victory." Dr. Dabney says that this was the only time that Jackson was ever heard to express joy at having gained the day.

When the surgeons came around him to dress his wounded hand he said, "No, I can wait; my wound is but a trifle; attend first to those poor fellows." He then sat down upon the grass and waited until the wounds of the badly hurt had been dressed. At first it was thought that his middle finger would have to be cut off, but Dr. McGuire having dressed it very skilfully, it was saved, and his hand at length healed.

It is stated by several friends that General Jackson said, while having his hand dressed, that, with ten thousand fresh troops, he believed that he could go into Washington city. However, as he was not the commanding general, he could not make the attempt, but could only do as he was ordered.

I must not fail to give you a part of a letter which he wrote to his wife the day after the battle, July 22nd:

"Yesterday we fought a great battle and gained a great victory, for which all the glory is due *to God alone*. Though under fire for several hours, I received only one wound, the breaking of the longest finger of the left hand, but the doctor says that it can be saved. My horse was wounded, but not killed. My coat got an ugly wound near the hip. * * * While great credit is due to other parts of our gallant army, God made my brigade more instrumental than any other in repulsing the main attack.

This is for you alone. Say nothing about it. Let another speak praise, not myself."

But the praise of the Stonewall Brigade was not sung by Jackson alone. Both friend and foe unite in saying that if Jackson had not held the hill, which was the key to the Confederate position, until help came, the battle of Manassas (Bull Run) would have been a defeat, and not a victory for the South.

Jackson's eagle eye saw the place to make a stand, and he held it for four hours against all odds.

At one time, while his men were lying upon the ground, they were so harassed by the bursting of shells that some of the officers begged to be permitted to advance. "No," said Jackson, "wait for the signal; *this place must be held*."

We do not seek to take glory from other heroes of this wonderful battle, many of whom, as Bee and Bartow, bravely gave up their lives in the storm of battle; or, as Smith and Early, made forced marches in order to rescue those so sorely pressed; but we do say that, in one sense, Jackson was the hero of the first battle of Manassas.

In this battle the Confederates captured twenty-eight cannon with five thousand muskets and vast stores of articles useful to their needy army.

The Confederates lost three hundred and sixty-nine killed on the field, and fourteen hundred and eighty-three wounded.

The road to Washington was now open, and there is no doubt that General Jackson thought it best to press on while the enemy was routed and take possession of the city.

But the commanding generals were afraid to risk the attempt with an army which had been drilled only a few weeks and which had so little discipline; and, thus, the moment to strike passed by.

In a few days the North had chosen a new commander, General McClellan, who set himself to raise new armies to defend Washington and to scourge the South.

Soon after the battle, General Jackson moved his men to a piece of woodland near by, where he employed the time in drilling his troops. After a time the Confederate lines were pushed forward to within sight of Washington city, but no battle took place, as General McClellan was too wise to risk another engagement so soon after Manassas.

In October, General Jackson was promoted to the rank of Major-General, and was sent to the Shenandoah Valley to take command of the army which had been fighting in West Virginia.

The Stonewall Brigade was left behind with General Johnston. This was a great trial, both to General Jackson and to the brigade.

When the time came for him to leave for the new field of war, he ordered the brigade to march out under arms, and then rode to their front with his staff. Dr. Dabney says that no cheer arose, but every face was sad.

After speaking a few words of praise and love, he threw his bridle reins on the neck of his horse, and stretching his arms towards them said: "In the Army of the Shenandoah, you were the First Brigade. In the Army of the Potomac, you were the First Brigade. In the Second Corps of the army, you are the First Brigade. You are the First Brigade in the affections of your General; and I hope, by your future deeds and bearing, you will be handed down to posterity as the First Brigade in this, our second War of Independence. Farewell."

He then waved his hand, and left the grounds at a gallop, followed by the cheers of his brave soldiers. This separation, however, was for but a short time. In November following, the First Brigade was ordered to join Jackson at Winchester, and it remained with him until the fatal hour at Chancellorsville, when it lost him forever.

Rüse (rooz), a trick.

Stáff, certain officers attached to an army.

Rout, fleeing in a confused and disorderly manner.

Ĭn'strū-mĕn'tăl, conducive to some end.

Dĭs'ciplĭne, order, rule.

Tell about—

General Johnston's army at Winchester.

Colonel Jackson's first battle in the Civil War.

The march to Manassas.

The first battle of Manassas.

Jackson's farewell to the Stonewall Brigade.

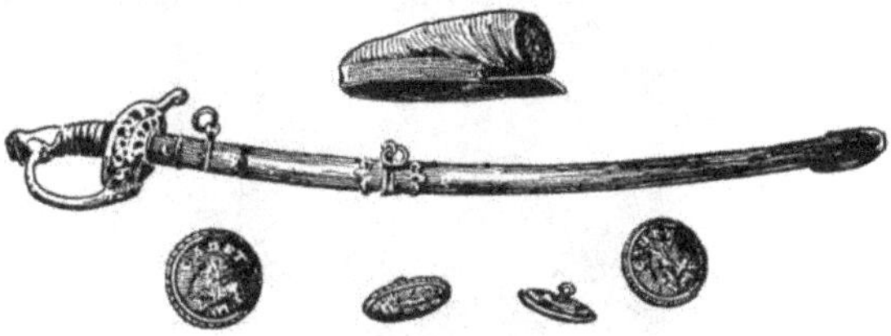

Jackson's military cap, sword, and buttons.

CHAPTER VII.
A Major-General.

When the year 1862 opened, General Jackson was at Winchester with ten thousand men, Generals Loring and Henry Jackson having come from Western Virginia to join his command.

At the head of Jackson's cavalry was Lieutenant-Colonel Ashby, a gallant, brave, and watchful officer. At the sound of his well-known shout and the cry of "Ashby," from his men, the Federal soldiers would turn and flee as if from a host. Ever guarding the outposts of the army, he was Jackson's "eyes and ears."

Lieut.-Col. Ashby.

There were now three great armies threatening Jackson, and he well knew that they would crush him if he did not meet each one singly before they could unite.

Jackson's little army was the guard to Johnston's flank. The latter general, with forty thousand men, was still at Manassas facing McClellan, who was at the head of an army of fifty thousand men, and preparing, as soon as spring opened, to "walk over Johnston."

Jackson knew that if his army was defeated, Johnston would have to retreat, and perhaps the whole State would be given up to the foe. The armies were now in winter quarters, and there was not much danger of a move before spring.

In the meantime, Jackson resolved to march against several large forces of Federals which were threatening him from the towns of Romney and Bath, forty miles distant, in Northwestern Virginia.

121

It was the last of December, however, before he could collect the men and supplies necessary for the expedition.

At last, on the first day of January, 1862, all was ready. The little army of about nine thousand men set out without knowing whither Jackson was leading, for he had not told even his officers his great plans.

In spite of the winter season, the day was bright and the air soft and balmy. So warm was the weather that the men left their overcoats and blankets to be brought on in the wagons. On the next day, a biting wind began to blow, which was followed by rain and snow.

The men marched all day, and at night the wagons, which had not been able to keep up with the troops, were still far behind. The troops rested that night without rations or blankets, having only camp-fires to keep off the cold.

On the third day, the men were so overcome by cold and hunger that they found it difficult to go forward. Jackson, riding grimly along the way, found his old brigade halted, and asked General Garnett the reason of the delay.

"I have halted," said General Garnett, "to let the men cook rations."

"There is not time for it," replied General Jackson curtly.

"But it is impossible for the men to go farther without them," said Garnett.

"I never found anything impossible with that brigade," said Jackson as he rode on. He was restive and eager to press forward; his plan to surprise the enemy did not admit of delay.

As the army neared the town of Bath, a force of Federals suddenly attacked it from behind trees and fences, but it was soon driven off with the loss of twenty prisoners.

That night the Southern troops went into camp just outside the town, in the midst of a heavy snow storm. The men were without food or blankets, and the wonder is how they lived through the night.

Jackson, however, did not change his plans, though there was great complaint among the men, many of whom straggled back to Winchester.

The next morning, after a hearty breakfast, the order was given to advance upon Bath. The artillery opened fire and the infantry charged the breastworks, but the Federals hastily gave up the town, and fled towards the Potomac river, which they waded that night.

The Southern troops on entering the town found quantities of stores which the Federals had left behind; among them were fine clothes, china, and even dinners, cooked and still smoking, ready to be eaten by the hungry Confederates.

From Bath, Jackson's men passed, with great difficulty and suffering, to a place called Hancock, about three miles distant from Bath, on the north side of the Potomac.

Jackson placed his cannon on the south bank and opened a hot fire on the town, but the commander refused to surrender. As a large force of men came up to reinforce the Federals, Jackson concluded to pass on to Romney.

In the meantime, the railroad bridge over Capon river had been destroyed and the telegraph wires cut by General Loring, so that the commander at Romney could not send to General Banks for help.

The weather had now become terrible. Rain, snow, sleet, and hail beat down upon men still without tents, overcoats, and blankets; for it was impossible for the wagons to come up. The mountain roads were covered with ice and sleet so that horses and men could not keep their footing. Many fell flat, badly hurt, while wagon after wagon slid down the steep banks, and was overturned and broken.

Jackson was everywhere along the line cheering the troops and even helping them along. We are told by Cooke, our great Virginia writer, that, as Jackson was passing a point in the road where a piece of artillery had stalled, while a crowd of men were looking on without helping, he stopped, dismounted, and, without uttering a word, put his shoulder to the wheel. The men, shamed, came forward to take their places, the horses were whipped up, and the piece moved on.

After great hardships, the little army at last reached Romney, on the 14th of January, to find that the Federals had retreated, leaving behind them large military stores, which fell into the hands of the Confederates.

Even then, the name of Jackson was a terror to the foe. With a force much larger than Jackson's, and when he was more than a day's march distant, the Federals had fled and left the greater part of their baggage.

In sixteen days, he had driven the enemy out of his district, had rendered the railroad useless to the Federals for more than a hundred miles, and had captured arms enough to equip an army as large as his own. This he had done with the loss of four men killed and twenty-eight wounded.

Leaving General Loring at Romney with a portion of the army, Jackson hastened back to Winchester to watch the movements of General Banks, who was stationed, with a large army, near Harper's Ferry.

Upon his return, he found the whole country in an uproar over the expedition to Romney through the sleet and snow. Though no one could say that Jackson was not full of courage and devotion to the South, many said that he was cruel and not fit to be in command of an army. Some said that he was a madman; others, that he was without common sense. Another charge against him was that he was partial to the Stonewall Brigade, as he had brought it back with him to the comforts of a town, while he had left Loring's command in the mountains. The soldiers of the brigade were called "Jackson's Pet Lambs," and other like names.

Now, the truth was, that Loring's men were far more comfortable than those of the Stonewall Brigade; the former being ordered into huts, while the latter were in tents, three miles from Winchester.

Another charge against him was that he would tell his plans to no one. "It was his maxim," says Dabney, "that in war, mystery was the key to success." He argued that no man could tell what bit of news might not be of use to the foe, and therefore, that it was the part of wisdom to conceal everything.

This secrecy irritated his officers, and it must be said that some of them so far forgot their duty as soldiers as to treat General Jackson with disrespect.

Though all of these charges were known to Jackson, he took no notice of them, but was proceeding to connect Romney with Winchester by telegraph wires when, on January 31st, he received this order from Richmond: "Order Loring back to Winchester at once."

The cause of this order was that some of the officers at Romney had sent a petition to Richmond asking to be sent back to Winchester, as the position at Romney was, in their opinion, too much exposed.

General Jackson recalled the troops from Romney, but he was so angry at the way in which he had been treated by the government, that he at once resigned his command.

This caused great excitement in the army and in the State at large. The people were by no means willing to give up an officer who had shown so much courage and skill, and they begged him to withdraw his resignation. This he refused to do. He said that the government had shown, by the order, that it did not trust him, and that, if he was to be meddled with in that way, he could do no good. At last, however, a sort of an apology being made by the government, he quietly took up his duties again.

In a few days after General Loring left Romney, the Federals again took possession of that town and the country around. So all the efforts of Jackson and the trials of his soldiers were of no avail. This was a great blow to General Jackson, for Winchester was again exposed to the advance of the foe from four directions.

The plan for the invasion of Virginia in 1862 was the same as in 1861. General Fremont was marching from the Northwest; Banks, from Harper's Ferry; McDowell, from Fredericksburg; McClellan faced Johnston at Manassas, and another large army was at Fortress Monroe, ready to march up the Peninsula.

The Northern army was much larger than the year before, but the Southern army was smaller, as the time of many of the men had expired and others had gone home on furlough.

Several brigades were now taken from General Jackson to strengthen other points, and he found himself left, with only six thousand men, to guard the left of Johnston's army and to protect the great Shenandoah Valley.

On the 26th of February, General Banks, with thirty-five thousand men, and General Kelly, with eleven thousand, advanced against Jackson, who was still at Winchester, hoping to hold that place, until help could come from General Johnston. But finding out through Colonel Ashby that he was almost surrounded by the enemy, he left Winchester and fell back slowly to Mt. Jackson, a village on the great turnpike, forty miles from Winchester. Here, he had sent all of his stores and sick soldiers some weeks before; so that, when the Federals entered Winchester, they found not a prisoner or a musket to "enrich their conquest."

It was a great trial to Jackson to leave his kind friends in Winchester, but he promised them "to wait for a better time and come again." We shall see how well he kept his promise.

On March 19th, General Johnston wrote to General Jackson at Mt. Jackson, asking him to move closer to the enemy and to prevent him, if possible, from sending troops across to McClellan. Word was brought at the same time, that fifteen thousand men were then leaving the army of Banks to aid in turning the left wing of Johnston's forces, as he fell back to lines of defense nearer Richmond.

So Jackson gave orders to his little army, which now numbered only twenty-seven hundred men, to march back down the Valley. That night the infantry slept at Strasburg, while Ashby's men drove in the outposts of the Federals at Winchester.

General Banks, thinking that Jackson would trouble him no more, had left for Washington, and General Shields was in command of the army.

General Jackson, on the morning of March 23rd, pushed forward his whole force, and, when about five miles from Winchester, at a place called Kernstown, he found Ashby fighting furiously with the advance of the foe. Taking a good position, he at once gave battle, though he saw that he was greatly outnumbered. The battle raged from about noon until night. Regiment after regiment was hurled against Jackson's thin ranks, but they fought stubbornly and would have gained the day, had not the ammunition of the Stonewall Brigade given out. Hearing his fire dying away for want of ammunition, General Garnett gave orders for his men to retreat. When Jackson saw the lines of his old brigade give back, he galloped to the spot, and, ordering Garnett to hold his ground, pushed forward to rally the men. Seeing a drummer boy retreating like the rest, he seized him by the shoulder, dragged him in full view of the soldiers, and said in his sternest tones, "Beat the rally!" The drummer beat the rally, and in the midst of a storm of balls Jackson saw the lines reform.

"Beat the Rally!"

But it was too late. The enemy now pressed forward in such numbers that there was nothing left to do but to retreat. This they did in good order, but the Federals held the field of battle where so many dead and wounded men were lying.

In this battle of Kernstown twenty-seven hundred Confederates, with eleven guns attacked eleven thousand Federals and almost gained the victory. It is said that General Shields had just given orders for his men to retreat when the Stonewall Brigade fell back.

As General Shields followed Jackson up the Valley after the battle, he stopped at a noted country house for the night. General Jackson had also rested there upon his retreat, and from his adjutant the lady of the house had learned the correct number of Jackson's men.

General Shields, at breakfast, entered into a conversation with his hostess, and in a polite way boasted of his great victory. "Ah! General," said the lady, "we can afford such defeats as that, when twenty-seven hundred men hold back eleven thousand for hours and then retreat at leisure! Such defeats are victories." General Shields was surprised to learn the small number of Jackson's forces, and begged the lady to tell him her informant. "Certainly," said the lady, "General Jackson's adjutant, Major Paxton. I have also information that large reinforcements are coming to Jackson and that he will again be ready to meet you." "I have no doubt of that, my dear Madam," smilingly returned the General.

Major E. F. Paxton.

That night Jackson's little army rested near Newtown, while Ashby kept watch not far from the field of battle. "Jackson," says Cooke, "got an armful of corn for his horse; and, wrapping his blanket about him, lay down by a fire in a fence corner and went to sleep." Though defeated for the first and last time, he had won the object of the battle. The fifteen thousand men who had started across the mountains to McClellan were recalled to the Valley, and Johnston was able to move safely behind the Rappahannock river, his new line of defense.

At four o'clock on the morning of the 24th, Jackson began to retreat slowly and in good order. The enemy pursued for awhile, but at last fell back to Winchester.

Jackson's army was far from cast down by the defeat at Kernstown. The soldiers felt that they had made a splendid fight against four times their number. And now, too, for the first time, it began to dawn upon them that their general was a great leader. As Jackson passed along the columns, the men would cheer themselves hoarse.

Cooke tells us that one man was heard to ask, as he struggled along, "Why is Old Jack a better general than Moses?" "Because it took Moses forty years to lead the Israelites through the wilderness, and Old Jack would have double-quicked them through it in three days!"

It is said by another writer, that the men would laugh and say that the only rest they had was when they were retreating before the enemy. He always led them by forced marches when going to attack the foe, but never fast enough on a retreat to lose the chances of a fight.

The weather was now mild and balmy, and the men suffered few hardships during their slow retreat. At last they reached the old camp at Mt. Jackson, where Jackson gathered up his wounded and sent them up the Valley.

On the 1st of April, he crossed the north fork of the Shenandoah, and took position on Rude's Hill, five miles below New Market.

General Banks had again come up the Valley, and was pressing upon the rear of Jackson's army.

It was left for Colonel Ashby to burn the bridge near Mt. Jackson, after the Southern army had passed over. While Ashby and his men were engaged in this work, the Federal cavalry dashed up and a skirmish ensued, in which Ashby's beautiful snow-white charger was mortally wounded.

General Jackson remained at Rude's Hill until April 17th, when, the waters having subsided so that the Federal army could cross the river, he again took up his line of march through New Market to Harrisonburg. At the last named place he turned east, and, passing the south end of Massanutton mountain, crossed the south branch of the Shenandoah river and posted his troops in the gorge of the Blue Ridge called Swift Run Gap.

The way to Staunton was now open to General Banks, but he was too timid to go forward. Jackson in his rear was worse than Jackson in front of him. So, for two weeks, Jackson held the Gap while Banks occupied Harrisonburg, and laid waste the country around.

Jackson had now about eight thousand men and thirty guns. His men had returned from hospitals and furloughs and also a number of new recruits had poured in to help in this time of danger. The General employed these weeks of rest in organizing and drilling his men and in mending up his old artillery. In the meantime also, he made bold plans, and with the help of General R. E. Lee, who had now been made commander of the "Army of Northern Virginia," proceeded to carry them out.

Now, in order to understand the great genius of our hero, and the bravery and endurance of his men, you must study the map on the next page.

You will see that the Valley of the Shenandoah is bounded on the east by the Blue Ridge mountains, and on the west by the Alleghany. Winchester is situated in the northern part of the Valley, while Staunton is about ninety miles to the south. These two places are connected by a fine turnpike.

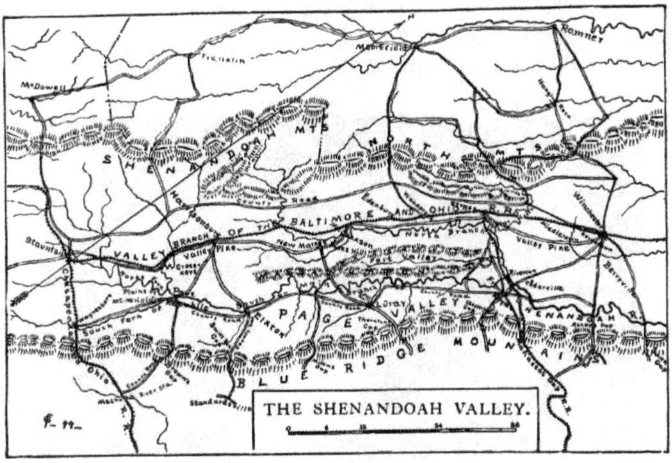

THE SHENANDOAH VALLEY

Now, near the center of the Valley, rises a beautiful mountain which the Indians called Massanutton, and which still retains that name. This mountain begins near Strasburg and extends about fifty miles towards Staunton, ending abruptly not far from Harrisonburg.

There is only one gap in the Massanutton mountain, and that is opposite the towns of New Market and Luray.

The valley east of the mountain is called the Page Valley, while the entire valley, including the Page Valley, is the Shenandoah Valley.

Some of the children who will read this book live under the shadow and in sight of this lovely mountain, which enabled Jackson to play at "hide and seek" with his foe, and I hope they will understand thoroughly the great movements which I shall relate.

Though Jackson and his little army were safe in Swift Run Gap, opposite the village of Elkton, for awhile, they could not have remained there long, as three major-generals, with as many large armies, were marching to surround and crush them. Banks was only fifteen miles distant, Milroy was coming by way of Staunton from Western Virginia, and Fremont from the northwest. General McDowell, at Fredericksburg, was also ordered to send twenty thousand men to the Valley, instead of advancing to help McClellan, who was now near Richmond with a large army. You see, Jackson was bravely obeying General Johnston's orders to keep the Federals busy in the Valley and to prevent them from reinforcing McClellan.

Now, there was a small force of Confederates, under General Edward Johnson, on Shenandoah mountain, twenty miles west of Staunton. There was great danger that Milroy with his larger army would overcome Johnson, take Staunton, and march on to join Banks. Their two armies would then be large enough to crush Jackson.

Generals Jackson, Johnston, and Lee.

It was also important to keep Staunton out of the hands of the foe, as it was situated on the Chesapeake and Ohio railway, which carried supplies from the fertile Valley to Richmond.

So General Jackson wrote to General Lee that he would go to the help of Johnson and protect Staunton, if he (Lee) would send a force to hold Banks in check during his absence.

This General Lee did, sending from Richmond General Ewell (ū'-el), a brave officer, with eight thousand men, who marched into Swift Run Gap from the east and took the places which Jackson's men had just left.

It was now Jackson's object to reach Staunton without the knowledge of Banks, so he marched, with great difficulty, through miry roads, down the mountain about eight miles to another gap across the Blue Ridge, called Brown's Gap. When there, he turned east and marched swiftly across the mountain into Albemarle county, passing through the village of White Hall to Mechum's River Station. Thence the troops were carried swiftly by rail to Staunton, reaching there on the night of the 4th of May, to the great joy of the people of Staunton, who thought that they had been deserted by Jackson in their time of need.

By Monday the whole army had come up. They were then joined by General Johnson and his army. On the 7th, one day having been spent in preparing for the march, Jackson, with General Johnson's command in front, marched towards Milroy, who was now posted on Shenandoah mountain.

Jackson had been joined at Staunton by the corps of cadets from the Military Institute at Lexington under Col. Scott Shipp. Many of them were mere boys, but they were filled with joy at taking their first look at grim war under Stonewall Jackson, who had so lately been a professor in that school.

As the Confederate army approached Shenandoah mountain, the Federals retreated to the village of McDowell.

On Thursday, May 8th, Jackson and Johnson, with the command of the latter still in advance, climbed the sides of the mountain overlooking that little village.

That evening, while the generals were waiting for the rest of the army to come up, General Milroy made an attack upon their position.

Though not expecting an attack, Jackson quickly placed his troops for the conflict, the center of the line being held by the Twelfth Georgia regiment with great bravery. It is related that, when ordered at one time to retire behind the crest of the hill to escape the raking fire of the foe, they refused to do so, and kept their position. The next day a tall youth from the Georgia regiment was asked why they did not fall back as ordered. He replied, "We did not come all the way to Virginia to run before Yankees."

The Twelfth Georgia Regiment at McDowell.

Just before the close of the battle, General Johnson was wounded in the ankle and compelled to leave the field.

The battle of McDowell raged from half-past four to half-past eight P. M., the shades of night closing the conflict. Then the Federals gave up the assault and retreated from the field. "By nine o'clock," says Dr. Dabney, "the roar of the struggle had passed away, and the green battle-field reposed under the starlight as calmly as when it had been occupied only by its peaceful herds of cattle."

It was one o'clock A. M. before General Jackson reached his tent, having waited to see the last wounded man brought off the battle-field, and the last picket posted. He had eaten nothing since morning, but when his faithful servant, Jim, came with food, he said, "I want none—nothing but sleep"; and in a moment he was fast asleep.

He was in the saddle at peep of day; but, upon climbing the mountain, he saw that the enemy had left during the night. He at once sent this dispatch to Richmond: "God blessed our arms with victory at McDowell yesterday," and then set out in pursuit of the fleeing Federals. He had followed them as far as Franklin, when the woods were set on fire by the Federals to conceal their position.

The dense smoke hung like a pall over the mountain roads, and the heat from the blazing forests was terrible. But still, the long column pressed on until Monday, when General Jackson received an order from General Lee to return to the Valley and pay his respects to General Banks, who was now at Strasburg.

When the latter general had found out that Ewell was holding the Swift Run Gap, and that Jackson had left to go—no one knew whither—he left Harrisonburg and retreated to Strasburg. Jackson was lost, and, not knowing where he might next appear, General Banks thought it more prudent to take a safer position.

Time was now precious to Jackson; so, after halting for a brief rest, during which time the whole army met to render thanks to God for the great victory, he set out on his return march to the Valley.

On the 20th, he was again in New Market, where he was joined by General Ewell.

By a bold plan and a swift march he had saved the army of General Johnson, and prevented Milroy from taking Staunton and joining Banks, and now he was again in pursuit of the latter.

General Banks was fortifying at Strasburg, and seemed to expect an attack in front, so Jackson wisely planned to attack him in the rear.

You remember that I told you that just east of New Market there is a pass, or gap, through the Massanutton mountain. Now Jackson sent a small force of cavalry down the turnpike towards Strasburg to hold it, and conceal the movements of the main army, which he himself led eastward across the mountain into the Page Valley.

Hidden by the friendly mountain, his troops marched quickly and silently to the town of Front Royal, which is at the northern end of the mountain, and which then guarded the flank of Banks' army.

So swift and silent had been the march, that Jackson's men were nearly in sight of the town before anyone knew of their presence.

One mile and a half from the town, the pickets were driven in, and an instant advance was ordered. The Confederate troops rushed to the attack. The Federals, thinking that Jackson was at least one hundred miles away, in the mountains of Western Virginia, were taken completely by surprise. They surrendered by hundreds, giving up quantities of valuable stores, among which were five hundred new revolvers and a wagon load of coffee.

The people of Front Royal were wild with joy at seeing the Confederates again, but the troops were not permitted to stop. On through the town they went at a double-quick, for the Federals had now made a stand outside of the town. But they were speedily put to flight, and the pursuit went on.

In the meantime, the Confederate cavalry came upon a body of Federals near Cedarville, five miles from Front Royal. A charge was at once made upon the Federals by the Confederates, and the whole force was driven back. The Federals then reformed in an orchard, and were again charged upon by the Confederates, and, after a fierce contest, were captured.

As night came on, the weary Southern troops went into camp, for they were quite worn out with marching and fighting.

The next morning, May 24th, the troops were again moving by peep of day. Our hero himself rode forward towards Middletown. When in sight of the turnpike which leads from Strasburg to Winchester, he saw long lines of Federal horsemen in full retreat.

Confederate Cavalry charge at Cedarville.

The batteries of Poague and Chew were brought forward and a hot fire opened upon the retreating foe. The latter broke in wild confusion, and soon the turnpike was filled with a mass of struggling and dying horses and men. A few regiments which formed the rear guard fell back to Strasburg, and, leaving their baggage at that place, fled through the western mountains to the Potomac river.

On the turnpike, Ashby with his cavalry followed closely after the fleeing foe, firing upon them with shot and shell.

Cooke says: "Either a shell or a round shot would strike one of the wagons and overturn it, and before those behind could stop their headway, they would thunder down on the remains of the first. Others would tumble in so as to block up the road; and in the midst of it all, Ashby's troopers would swoop down, taking prisoners or cutting down such as resisted."

Ashby himself pressed forward, and at one time, it is said, took as many as thirty prisoners, unaided and alone.

But Ashby's men soon betook themselves to plundering the wagons, which were rich in stores, and thus gave the enemy time to recover from their panic. When near Newtown, the enemy turned and fired upon their pursuers.

At dark, however, the firing ceased, and Jackson himself went forward to urge on the pursuit.

The main body of the army had now come up, but no halt was made for food or rest. The "foot cavalry" of the Valley marched all night along the pike lit up by "burning wagons, pontoon bridges, and stores."

Every now and then, they would come upon men ambuscaded along the sides of the pike, and fierce fights would ensue.

About dawn on the 25th of May, Jackson's advance force climbed the lofty hill southwest of Winchester. This hill was already held by the Federals, but they were charged upon by the Stonewall Brigade, and driven back. With a loud shout the Confederates gained the crest of the hill and planted their batteries. Though they had marched all night, they took no rest or food, but at once began the battle of Winchester.

Ewell fought on the right and Taylor on the left. "Jackson," says a writer, "had his war-look on, and rode about the field, regardless of shot and shell, looking as calm as if nothing were going on."

At last, after a fierce fight, the Federals gave way, and Jackson entered Winchester at the heels of the panic-stricken army. The people of the town were beside themselves with delight to see their loved general once more.

Jackson was for the first time excited. He waved his faded cap around his head and cheered with a right good will.

But the troops still pressed forward, Jackson leading the way. When one of his officers said, "Don't you think you are going into too much danger, General?" his reply was, "Tell the troops to press right on to the Potomac."

And they did press onward until the enemy was forced across the Potomac with the loss of many prisoners and valuable stores.

After resting a few days, Jackson advanced towards Harper's Ferry with the view of attacking the Federal force there, but was stopped by the news that two armies, one under General Shields, from the east; the other under General Fremont, from the west, were to meet at Strasburg and thus cut him off from Richmond and capture him.

He at once hastened back to Winchester, where he collected his prisoners and the stores of ammunition and medicine which he had captured. These he sent up the Valley, and followed rapidly with his whole army.

In the meantime, there was great terror at Washington and in the North. Men wore anxious faces, and were asking each other, "Where is Jackson?" They were afraid that he would turn and capture Washington.

But Jackson had only about fifteen thousand men, and he could not risk the loss of the rich stores which he had gained and the destruction of his noble army, so he put forth all his skill and nerve to save them.

The Confederates now began a race to reach Strasburg before the Federals, the larger part of the army marching from near Harper's Ferry to Strasburg, nearly fifty miles, in about twenty-four hours. Well might they be called the "foot cavalry."

As Jackson marched into Strasburg, General Fremont's advance was almost in sight; and, as the Stonewall Brigade had not yet come up, Jackson sent General Ewell to hold Fremont in check. A fierce battle ensued, but Ewell at last drove back the enemy, and the Stonewall Brigade coming up that evening, the whole army continued to retreat up the Valley.

The race had been won by Jackson, who was, for the present, safe. In a brief space of time, he had flanked the enemy at Front Royal, chased them to Middletown, beaten them at Winchester, and sent them flying across the Potomac. When nearly entrapped by two other columns, he had passed between them, and was now hurrying with his rich stores to the upper Valley. Cooke tells us that he had captured two thousand three hundred prisoners, one hundred cattle, thirty-four thousand pounds of bacon, salt, sugar, coffee, hard bread, and cheese, valuable medical stores, $125,185 worth of other stores, two pieces of artillery, and many small-arms and horses. All this was gained with the loss of about four hundred men.

But, as Jackson retreated up the Valley, he was again threatened by a great danger. Shields's column marched up the Page Valley with the view of crossing the Massanutton at New Market and striking Jackson in the rear, just as Jackson had done to Banks when he went down to Front Royal. But Jackson was too wary to be taken by surprise.

He sent swift horsemen across the mountain, who burned the bridges over the south branch of the Shenandoah at Columbia Mills and the White House, and then placed signal stations on top of the mountain to inform him of what was going on in the Page Valley.

Fremont was now pressing on his rear, but he moved swiftly up the Valley with the main army, while Ashby kept guard on every side. When Harrisonburg was reached, he again marched east and took his stand near the village of Port Republic.

On the 6th of June, as the gallant Ashby was leading a charge to repel the advance of the Federal forces, he fell, pierced to the heart by a single bullet. His last words were, "Charge, Virginians!" Thus, in the moment of victory, died the brave and noble Ashby. His loss was deeply felt by Jackson, who now needed more than ever, the daring and skill of his "Chief of Cavalry."

As I have told you, Jackson was at Port Republic, a village at the forks of the Shenandoah river. Fremont was at Harrisonburg, fifteen miles to the northwest, and Shields was at Conrad's Store, fifteen miles to the northeast. The space between the three generals formed the sides of a triangle. Just back of Jackson, in the Blue Ridge, was Brown's Gap, through which he could retreat and join Lee before Richmond.

But Jackson had no idea of leaving the Valley without a parting blow. The Shenandoah was very high, so that Shields and Fremont could not unite their forces. Jackson therefore determined to attack Shields first, and, if victorious, then to turn his attention to Fremont. I have forgotten to tell you that Shields was east of the river, and Fremont to the west; while Jackson was between the north and south branches of the Shenandoah, which unite at Port Republic. There was a bridge over the north branch, between Jackson and Fremont; but over the south branch, between Jackson and Shields, there was only a ford. The north bank was high, while the south was low, and stretched away in broad meadows towards the mountains.

Jackson, leaving the trusty Ewell at Cross Keys to watch Fremont, who was advancing from Harrisonburg, took possession of the heights overlooking the bridge at Port Republic, and stationed there two brigades and his remaining artillery. A small body of cavalry was sent across South river to find out the position of Shields.

General R. S. Ewell.

Early on the morning of the 8th of June, the cavalry came galloping back with the news that Shields's army was close at hand. Jackson, who was in the town with some of his staff, at once gave orders for the batteries on the north side to open fire; but before it could be done, the Federal cavalry dashed into the town followed by artillery, which rumbled forward and took position at the southern end of the bridge.

Jackson and his staff were now cut off from his army, which was on the north bank. We are told by Cooke and others that Jackson, with great presence of mind, rode towards the bridge; and, rising in his stirrups, called sternly to the Federal officer commanding the gun, "Who told you to post that gun there, sir? Bring it over here!" The officer, thinking that Jackson was a Federal general, bowed, "limbered up" the piece, and was preparing to move. In the meantime Jackson and his staff galloped across the bridge, and were soon safe on the northern side.

General Jackson at Port Republic Bridge.

No time was lost by the Confederates. Their artillery opened fire upon the Federals, and Jackson in person led the Thirty-seventh Virginia regiment, drove the foe from the bridge, and captured the gun with the loss of only two men wounded.

In the meantime, Jackson's long wagon-train, which contained his ammunition, was bravely defended on the outskirts of the village by a handful of pickets and a section of artillery until help came.

The fire of the guns on the north bank made it impossible for the Federals to hold the village, so, leaving their other gun, they retreated, and dashed across the ford of the South river by the way they had come.

Hardly had the guns stopped firing at Port Republic, before heavy firing was heard in the direction of Cross Keys, five miles off, between Ewell and Fremont. The latter had twenty thousand men, while Ewell had only about six thousand. The Confederates were posted with great skill upon a ridge, and after fighting from ten A. M. until nightfall, at last drove back the enemy with great loss.

The battle of Cross Keys having been fought, the Confederate troops lay upon their arms, ready to renew the fray the next day; but Jackson had other plans.

He had determined to strike Shields next; so, leaving a guard to watch Fremont, he ordered Ewell to march at break of day to Port Republic.

At midnight he caused a foot-bridge to be thrown across South river so that his infantry might pass over to attack Shields. This bridge was made by placing wagons lengthwise across the swollen stream. The floor of the bridge was formed of long boards laid loosely from one wagon to another. Over this rude, frail structure, the whole body of infantry passed, but not so quickly as its general wished. About midway the stream, for some reason, one wagon was about two feet higher than the next. This made a step, and all the boards on the higher wagon were loose but one. When the column began to move over, several men were thrown, by the loose planks, into the water; so, refusing to trust any but the firm plank, the men went, at this point, in single file. This made the crossing over very tedious; and, instead of being in line to attack Shields at sunrise, it was ten o'clock before the entire army had passed over. Thus, three loose boards cost the Confederates a bloody battle; for they found the Federals drawn up in battle array and ready for the fight. This incident shows how much care should be taken in performing the most trivial duty; as the success of great events is often affected by very slight causes. It is said that Jackson hoped to surprise Shields, whip him in a few hours, and then recross the river to rout Fremont.

But the battle of Port Republic, June 9th, raged furiously for hours. The Federals fought with great courage, and it was not until evening that they gave way and retreated, panic-stricken, from the field.

The Confederates followed them eight or ten miles down the river, and returned laden with spoils and prisoners.

At ten o'clock A. M., Jackson sent orders for the guard left at Cross Keys under General Trimble and Colonel Patton to march to his aid and to burn the bridge behind them. This they did, and came up in time to join in the fight.

Towards nightfall General Jackson led his weary troops by a side road into the safe recesses of Brown's Gap, in the Blue Ridge.

As they passed the field of battle on their return, they saw the hills on the north side of the river crowded with the troops of Fremont, who had arrived in time to see the rout of Shields.

The river being high, they did not attempt to cross, but began a furious cannonade upon the Confederate surgeons and men who were caring for the wounded and burying the dead.

The next day, scouts brought word to Jackson that Fremont was building a bridge, but soon after, having learned, doubtless, that General Shields's army was entirely routed, he retreated.

On June 12th, the Confederate cavalry under Colonel Munford entered Harrisonburg, Fremont having gone back down the Valley, leaving behind him his sick and wounded, and many valuable stores.

Four hundred and fifty Federals were taken prisoners on the field, while as many more were found in the hospitals. One thousand small-arms and nine field-pieces fell to the victorious Confederates. The Federal loss in the two battles was about two thousand. In the battle of Cross Keys Jackson lost only forty-two killed and two hundred and thirty-one wounded; but in the battle of Port Republic, ninety-one officers and men were killed, and six hundred and eighty-six wounded.

Though Jackson's plans had not been entirely carried out, he was now rid of the two armies of forty thousand men which had been on his front and flanks, and had threatened to crush him.

Within forty days his troops had marched four hundred miles, fought four great battles, and defeated four separate armies, sending to the rear over three thousand prisoners and vast trains of stores and ammunition.

From this time Jackson stood forth as a leader of great genius; the little orphan boy had indeed climbed the heights of fame amid a "blaze of glory."

On the 12th of June, Jackson led his army from its camp, in Brown's Gap, to the plains of Mt. Meridian, a few miles above Port Republic. Here, the wearied men rested for five days, while Colonel Munford, who now commanded the cavalry, kept watch on the turnpike below Harrisonburg.

This is the dispatch which Jackson sent to Richmond:

"NEAR PORT REPUBLIC, June 9th, 1862.

Through God's blessing, the enemy near Port Republic was this day routed, with the loss of six pieces of his artillery.

T. J. JACKSON, *Major-General, commanding.*"

The Saturday following the battle was set apart by General Jackson as a day of thanksgiving and prayer, and the next day (Sunday) the Lord's Supper was celebrated by the Christian soldiers from all the army. General Jackson was present at this service, and partook of the sacred feast in company with his men.

On the 16th of June, General Jackson ordered Colonel Munford to press down the pike, if possible, as far as New Market, and to make the enemy believe that his whole army was advancing. This Colonel Munford did, and the Federals, believing that Jackson was again on the march, retreated to Strasburg and began to fortify themselves.

In the meanwhile, June 17th, Jackson had begun a march, but not towards Strasburg. The mighty army of McClellan had advanced so close to Richmond that at night the reflection of its camp-fires could be seen from the city; and General Lee sent for Jackson to come to his aid as swiftly as possible.

Great care was taken to make the Federals believe that troops were being sent to Jackson, so that he could again go down the Valley, and attack Fremont and Shields at Strasburg. A division of men was sent as far as Staunton, and the report was spread that a large force was on the march to Jackson; but the truth was, that our hero was already on his way to Richmond, where the next blow was to be struck.

It was important to keep the Federals in ignorance of Jackson's movement, so Colonel Munford was ordered to make a great show with his men along the turnpike, and to allow no news to be carried to the foe. The men were told to give this answer to all questions, "I do not know." The historian Cooke tells us this amusing incident, which grew out of the above order: "One of Hood's men left the ranks to go to a cherry-tree near by, when Jackson rode past and saw him. 'Where are you going?' asked the General. 'I don't know,' replied the soldier. 'To what command do you belong?' 'I don't know.' 'Well, what State are you from?' 'I don't know.' 'What is the meaning of all this?' asked Jackson. 'Well,' was the reply, 'Old Stonewall and General Hood issued orders yesterday that we were not to know anything until after the next fight.' Jackson laughed and rode on."

On the 25th of June, the corps reached Ashland, near Richmond.

Jackson had gone on in advance to the headquarters of General Lee, where his post in the coming strife was assigned him.

Flăñk, side of an army or fleet.

Rē'ĭn-fōrce', to send more soldiers.

Mys'tery, a great secret.

Pētĭ'tion (pē-tish'-un), a request.

Gēn'ius (jēn'-yus), a man of wonderful mind.

Ăd'jutañt, a military officer who assists another.

Describe—

The battle of Kernstown.

The retreat to Swift Run Gap, McDowell, Front Royal, Winchester, Cross Keys, Port Republic.

The march to Richmond.

CHAPTER VIII.
A Major-General.
(CONTINUED.)

General McClellan was now on the banks of the Chickahominy river, at one point only six miles from Richmond, with the largest and best equipped army that had ever been raised upon American soil.

His position was a strong one, having the Pāmun'key river on one side and the James on the other, with the marshes of the Chickahominy in front as natural barriers to the assaults of the Confederates. Besides, he had thoroughly fortified his line, which swept in a crescent shape from Meadow Bridge road on the right, across the Chickahominy, to the Williamsburg road on the left—a distance of about fifteen miles.

General Lee now determined to send General Jackson to the rear of the enemy to turn their flank, while General A. P. Hill and Longstreet assailed them in front.

On the evening of the 26th of June, General A. P. Hill advanced upon Mechanicsville and attacked the strong position of the Federals. The latter defended themselves bravely, but at last fell back to their works on Beaverdam creek. The victorious Confederates followed, and an artillery fire was kept up until nine o'clock at night. The attack was renewed at dawn the next morning and raged for hours, when, suddenly, the Federals retreated in haste from their strong position, leaving everything in flames.

Gen. A. P. Hill.

Jackson had come up, turned their flank, and caused them to retire. Generals Hill and Longstreet followed them until about noon, when they found the Federals again drawn up for battle behind Powhite creek, on a ridge whose slope was fortified by breastworks of trees, and whose crest was crowned with batteries of frowning guns.

The Confederate troops at once advanced, but were repulsed with great loss. Again they charged up the hill, and gained the crest only to be driven back by the storm of shot and shell.

Longstreet was now ordered to make a move on the right towards Gaines's Mill, where the Federals were massed in a strong position. In the meanwhile General Lee ordered General Jackson to advance to the help of Hill. About five o'clock P. M. the sound of guns was heard to the left, and soon Jackson's corps was in the thickest of the fight.

Before them were a swamp, a deep stream, masses of felled timber, and a wood filled with armed men, and cannon belching forth shot and shell. The work was hard, but when Jackson gave the order, his men swept forward with wild cheers and a roar of musketry, while above the clang arose the cry of Jackson! Jackson! Jackson!

The men rushed on through the swamp, across the creek, and up into the wood, and drove the enemy from point to point until they gained the top of the hill.

On the right of the line, Hood's Texas brigade charged with a yell, leaped ditch and stream, and drove the foe pell-mell before them. In this charge they lost one thousand men, but took fourteen cannon and nearly a regiment of prisoners.

General J. B. Hood.

The enemy now retreated in wild disorder all along the line, and the battle of Old Cold Harbor was won by the Confederates. The very name of Jackson had struck terror to the foe!

The next morning, the 29th of June, Jackson was ordered to move on the rear of McClellan's army.

At Savage Station, the Confederates, under General Magruder, had a fierce fight with the rear guard of the Federals. At nightfall the latter again gave way, leaving behind vast stores and a number of wounded men. While the battle at Savage Station had been going on, the main body of the Federal army passed over the bridge at White Oak swamp, destroyed it, and were for awhile safe, for the Confederates could not pass over the marshy stream under the fire of the Federals, who were massed on the opposite bank.

General Jackson opened fire with his artillery, and the next morning, the 1st of July, forced the passage of White Oak swamp, and captured a part of the Federal artillery.

In the meantime a fierce battle had been fought at Frasier's farm, by Generals Longstreet and A. P. Hill, with another portion of McClellan's army. Under cover of night, the latter drew off, leaving his dead and wounded, and a large number of prisoners.

General Jackson was now placed in front of the Confederate forces in pursuit of the foe, who was nearing the James river. It was General Lee's plan to cut them off from the river and destroy the whole army, but the Confederates were worn out with much fighting, and General McClellan was allowed to make a stand on Malvern Hill. This strong position he had hastily fortified; and here, as a wild animal at bay, was his whole army, determined to contend for existence.

General Lee ordered an assault, placing Jackson and D. H. Hill on the left and Magruder on the right. Owing to the timber and marshes, the Confederates could use but little artillery, while the Federals, from their greater height, rained a storm of shot and shell from three hundred cannon. The gunboats on the James also threw their monstrous shells above the heads of the Confederates. In spite of all odds, these devoted men (Jackson's) charged across marshes and up the hill, forcing the enemy back; but, after a fierce combat, they fell back with great loss. Again and again they charged, with the same result. At sunset, Magruder, who with much difficulty had gotten his troops into position, charged on the right with great bravery.

As darkness came on, the Confederates fought with renewed courage. Whole lines of the enemy fell beneath their musket fire, but the guns could not be taken by the Confederates, because no line of men could live within the zone of fire which flamed from the mouths of the blazing cannon.

About ten o'clock P. M. the firing ceased, and the Confederate troops, holding their position, slept upon the battle-field.

When the battle had ended thus, Jackson went slowly to the rear, where his faithful servant, Jim, was waiting for him with food and a pallet made upon the ground. After eating a few morsels, Jackson lay down and fell into a deep sleep. About one o'clock, Generals Hill, Ewell, and Early came to tell him that their commands were cut to pieces, and that when day broke they would not be able to continue the fight. Jackson listened to them in silence, and then said: "McClellan and his army will be gone by daylight." The generals thought him mad, but when morning came, they found that he had foretold aright the flight of McClellan. Malvern Hill was found to be deserted by the foe. They had retreated during the night to Harrison's landing, under cover of their gunboats, and Richmond was for the time safe.

The battle of Malvern Hill was a dearly bought victory for the Confederates. General Jackson lost in the battle three hundred and seventy-seven men killed, and one thousand seven hundred and forty-six wounded, with thirty nine missing. As soon as possible, the Southern army followed McClellan, but found him too strongly entrenched to attack. So the worn-out men went into camp near by, and rested for the first time in a fortnight.

General Jackson soon grew weary of watching McClellan, and began to plan a bold march into Maryland to threaten Washington city. It was not long before he did move northward. News came that a Federal army of forty thousand men, under General Pope, was coming towards Gordonsville to the help of McClellan. General Jackson was at once ordered to advance to meet him and drive him back.

His corps moved forward, and, on August 9th, fought the battle of Cedar Run. In this fierce battle one of the regiments began to fall back. At that instant Jackson placed himself in front of his men, drew his sword, and cried in a voice of thunder, "Rally, brave men! Jackson will lead you! Follow me!" This turned the tide of battle, and the Federal army broke into full retreat. Just before this battle, some officers enquired of "Jim," the General's servant, if there were any signs of a battle. "Oh, yes, sir," replied he, "the General is a great man for praying night and morning, all times; but when I see him get up in the night and go off and pray, then I know there is going to be something to pay; and I go right straight and pack his haversack, for I know he will call for it in the morning."

General Lee now came up with the greater part of the Southern army, leaving only a small force to watch General McClellan. The plan of the Southern leaders was to rout General Pope and march northward to threaten Washington, thus compelling General McClellan to leave his camp on the James river.

The main body of Lee's army moved nearer to Pope's front, while Jackson's corps moved off to the northwest, and was again "lost." It was marching across the Rappahannock and behind Bull Run mountains, which hid it from the enemy.

General Jackson preparing for battle.

On August 26th it passed through the mountains at Thoroughfare Gap, and took a position between Pope and Washington city.

Jackson at once took Manassas Junction, where three hundred prisoners and immense quantities of stores were captured. The poor, hungry soldiers took what could be carried away, and the rest was burned.

As soon as Pope heard that Jackson was in his rear, he moved to meet him, and ordered McDowell to close in upon him from the direction of Gainesville, saying, "We shall bag the whole crowd." But the wary Jackson was a match for his foes. Taking a good position upon the old battle-field of Manassas, he at once attacked the enemy coming up on the evening of August 28th. When darkness fell upon the blood-drenched plain, the

Confederates were the victors. On the next morning the fight was renewed, but Jackson's men were almost exhausted, when Longstreet's corps appeared and soon turned the tide of battle.

It was not long before Pope's army was in full retreat towards Washington, and Jackson was again victor. During a part of the battle a severe storm came up. An aide from General A. P. Hill rode up, and reported that his ammunition was wet, and asked leave to retire. "Give my compliments to General Hill," said Jackson, "and tell him that the Yankee ammunition is as wet as his; to stay where he is." "There was always blood and danger," says a friend, "when Jackson began his sentences with, 'Give my compliments.'"

General Lee now determined to cross the Potomac and threaten Washington, and Jackson led the advance. On September 6th he reached Frederick and remained there several days, resting and refitting his command. When General Lee came up, he at once sent General Jackson to Harper's Ferry (September 10th), to capture the Federal forces at that place. After taking the heights around that town, he proceeded to take the town by storm.

In a short while the garrison of eleven thousand men, with seventy-three cannon, thirteen thousand stand of small-arms and a vast amount of stores, surrendered. Jackson, leaving General Hill to receive the captured prisoners and property, at once set out to return to General Lee, at Sharpsburg, a little village two and one-half miles from the Potomac river. After a weary night-march he reached that place on the morning of the 16th. He found General Lee facing the hosts of McClellan and drawn up for battle. When he had rested his worn-out men for several hours, he took his position on the left, next to the Potomac river. This was the post of danger, for against it, on the 17th, McClellan massed forty-four thousand men.

The corps of Jackson numbered now, after so much fighting and marching, less than seven thousand men, but this little band held the ground throughout the day, and bravely drove back every assault of the enemy.

When night closed the bloody fray, each army held its own position. On the next morning, General Lee awaited another attack, but General McClellan had received so heavy a blow that he would not venture another battle until fresh troops had come up.

The 18th was spent by both armies in burying their dead and caring for the wounded. In the evening General Lee, learning that large bodies of fresh troops were reaching McClellan, determined to recross the Potomac. As soon as night came, the troops began to move towards the ford at Shepherdstown. "For hours," says Dr. Dabney, "Jackson was seen seated upon his horse, motionless as a statue, watching the passage until the last man and the last carriage had touched the Southern shore." The battle of Sharpsburg, or Antietam (An tē'tam), as it is sometimes called, was a drawn battle—neither side was victorious, each losing in killed and wounded about twelve thousand men.

The Southern men were so worn out and foot-sore from constant marching, and weak from starvation, that they were really unfit for the battle of Sharpsburg. More than half of Lee's army was left behind along the Virginia roads, and those who, wan and gaunt, fought the battle, were kept up during that bloody day only by their devotion to the Southern cause and leaders. Fortune also had smiled upon McClellan by revealing to him the plans of Lee. An order setting forth Lee's line of march was picked up in D. H. Hill's deserted camp, and taken to McClellan, who then, of course, knew just where to strike Lee.

On the morning of the 19th, a force of Federals crossed the Potomac at Boteler's ford, but were met by A. P. Hill's division of Jackson's corps, and driven back into the river with great loss. On the northern side of the river, seventy large cannon were planted, which rained grape-shot upon the Southern men, but they rushed forward and hurled hundreds of the Federals into the water, and then picked them off with steady aim until the river was black with floating bodies.

While this was going on, a messenger from General Lee found Jackson watching the progress of the fight. His only remark was, "With the blessing of Providence, they will soon be driven back." McClellan made no further attempt to follow Lee.

For some weeks Lee's army lay quietly resting in the lower Valley. But Jackson was never idle. He was now busy in getting clothes and shoes for his men, and filling up the ranks which had been so thinned during the summer. His regiments were at the time filled up by the return of the sick and the foot-sore and by new recruits.

Jackson had now become the idol of his men. Their pet name for him was "Old Jack." Whenever he rode by they would cheer themselves hoarse; and his devotion to them was just as great. This story is told of him by an eye-witness of the scene: "When Jackson's men were on their famous march to Manassas, at the close of the first day, they found Jackson, who had ridden forward, dismounted, and standing upon a great stone by the road-side. His sun-burned cap was lifted from his brow and his blue eyes gleamed in the rays of the setting sun. His men burst forth into cheers, but he at once sent an officer to request that there be no cheering, as it might betray their presence to the enemy. Instantly the cheering stopped, but as they passed their General their eyes told what their lips could not utter—their love for him. Jackson turned to his staff, his face beaming with delight, and said,

'Who could not conquer with such troops as these?'" Well might he be proud of men who had been marching and fighting for five days, many of them having no rations and living upon green corn found along the way, yet whose courage and devotion knew no bounds!

Crĕs'çent, shaped like the new moon.

Băr'rier, a bar, a defense.

Swamp, soft, low, and spongy ground.

De-vō'-tion, love.

Re-vēal-ing, making known.

Can you describe—

McClellan's position on the Chickahominy river?

The charge of Jackson's men at "Old Cold Harbor"?

The battle of Malvern Hill?

The second battle of Manassas?

The capture of Harper's Ferry?

The battle of Antietam?

CHAPTER IX.
A Lieutenant-General.

While our hero was in the lower Valley, on the 11th of October, 1862, the Confederate Government bestowed upon him the rank of Lieutenant-General, next to the highest grade in the service. General Lee's army was now divided into two great corps, one of which was given to Jackson, the other to Longstreet. These generals have been called the "two hands" of Lee.

On the 18th of October, General Jackson's corps was sent forward to destroy the Baltimore and Ohio railroad. This they did in the most complete way. Burning all the bridges and ripping up the cross-ties, they finished their work by setting fire to the ties and throwing the iron rails upon the heaps of blazing logs.

After the work was done, Jackson rode over the whole distance, thirty miles, to see that the destruction was complete.

Towards the end of October, Jackson moved his corps near the Blue Ridge mountains to watch the movements of McClellan, who was again crossing the Potomac with a vast army of one hundred and forty thousand men.

General James Longstreet.

But McClellan's movements were so slow that he was removed from his command, and General Burnside was put in his place.

The latter general resolved to try a new way to Richmond, and moved his army towards Fredericksburg, on the Rappahannock river. General Lee at once marched to that town to meet him. General Jackson was called from the Valley to the help of Lee, and reached that general's camp on the 1st of December. The Southern army numbered in all about sixty-five thousand men. Of these, there were in Jackson's corps twenty-five thousand.

General Lee, with his two corps, was now upon the heights south of the Rappahannock river; while General Burnside, with five corps, held Stafford Heights, north of that river. The town of Fredericksburg was between the two armies. The winter set in early, and both armies suffered greatly from the cold. The Confederates were for the most part barefooted, without tents and warm clothes, and had only rations of fat meat and corn bread; but these trials did not lessen their valor. They dug out trenches and threw up breastworks, and waited for the advance of the enemy.

On the 10th of December, General Burnside began to move his men over the river on pontoon bridges. One hundred and fifty big guns on Stafford Heights poured shot and shell upon the town of Fredericksburg, setting it on fire and causing many of the people to leave their homes. By the morning of the 13th, ninety thousand Federals had crossed the river. Longstreet held the Confederate left while Jackson held the right.

The battle began by a fierce attack upon Jackson's right, which onset was bravely met; for the men, fighting fiercely, drove the Federals back to the cover of their big guns. At eleven A. M., the Federals assaulted Longstreet's position, but again and again they were driven back by the Confederates, who did not fire until the foe was close upon them. Charge after charge was made by the Federals, but to no purpose, for the grim Confederates held their own.

When night came, thirteen thousand Federals lay dead or wounded upon the frozen plain, while the Confederates had lost five thousand brave men.

There is no doubt that Jackson ordered a night attack upon Burnside's beaten army, hoping thereby to turn a defeat into a rout, and to drive them pell-mell into the river, as he had done at Boteler's ford; but his better judgment told him that it was unwise to send his men against the strong works along the river road, under the fierce fire of the cannon on Stafford Heights.

So he recalled the order, and thus lost the chance of a decisive victory; for Burnside did not offer battle again, but on the night of the 16th, in the midst of a great storm of wind and rain, withdrew his forces to their post on Stafford Heights.

Both armies now went into winter quarters. Jackson's corps built huts in the forests, and made themselves as comfortable as possible, while their

General accepted for his lodgings a cottage at Moss Neck, the home of Mr. Corbin.

Here he set to work to write out reports to the government of his wonderful battles. This he did with great clearness and regard for the truth, recording briefly the exploits of his little army.

Never had general a more glorious story to relate!

Since the battle of Kernstown, in March, these brave men had fought the big battles of McDowell, Cross Keys, Port Republic, Cold Harbor, Malvern Hill, Cedar Run, Manassas, Harper's Ferry, Antietam, and Fredericksburg—marched hundreds of miles, and captured thousands of prisoners. Never had they quailed in battle; when ammunition had given out they fought with stones, and when there had been no rations, they lived on roots and berries. So rapidly did they march from place to place that they were called the "foot cavalry," and the knowledge that Jackson was "lost," cast terror into the ranks of the toe. Even their best generals could not tell where Jackson would next be found.

"During the battle of Cold Harbor," relates one of Jackson's men, "as we were taking back some prisoners, one of them said: 'You think that you are doing great things here, but I tell you we are whipping "Old Jack" in the Valley like smoke.' 'Well, maybe you are,' said I, 'being as "Old Jack" is *here*. You've been fighting his men all day.'"

Just then, Jackson rode by with his staff. "There's our General," said I; "now, how much are you whipping us in the Valley?" The man looked dazed, and said, "Well, my stars, if that *ain't* 'Old Jack!'"

Indeed, the feats of Jackson had now made him famous. Not only his own people, but strangers from Europe made visits to the camp to see the great general and his men.

During these months of rest, Jackson enjoyed greatly the visits of General Stuart, who made the mess merry with his jokes and gay laughter. He also made the acquaintance of little six-year-old Jane Corbin, who lived near by in the big house.

Every evening when the work of the day was over, she would run across to see the General, who would always have some little present for her. One evening, having no other gift for her, he ripped off the one band of gold braid from around his new cap, and placed it upon her sunny brow.

This lovely child lived only a few months thereafter. The very day on which General Jackson left Moss Neck in the spring, little Jane was seized with scarlet-fever and died after being ill only one day. General Jackson mourned greatly for his little friend. About the same time he heard of the illness of his own baby daughter, whom he had never seen.

He had never had a furlough since leaving Lexington, and in April, since he could not visit his dear ones, they came to him. He found a quiet home for his wife near by, and great was his pleasure in nursing and caressing his little daughter. He gave her his mother's name—Julia.

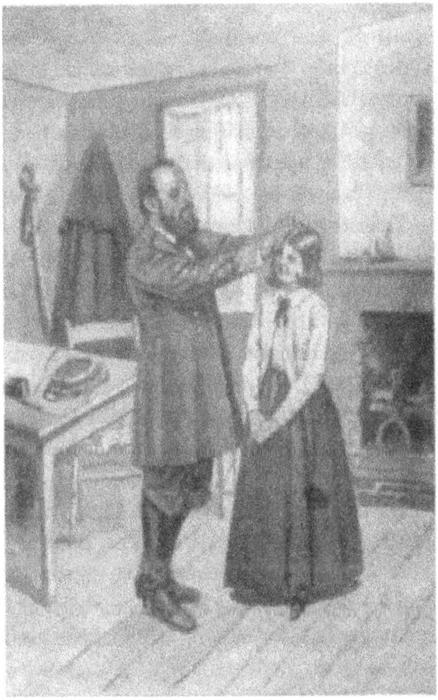

General Jackson crowning Jane Corbin.

During the winter, at Moss Neck, the piety of General Jackson seemed ever to increase. His chief thought was to live for the glory of God. He often worshiped with his men in the log church which they had built in the forest, and toiled early and late for their welfare.

Cooke, the historian, tells us that one day, while talking with a member of his staff about the great battle which he knew would soon take place, he said: "My trust is in God." A brief silence followed these words, and then, rising to his feet, he exclaimed, with flashing eyes, "I wish they would come."

The spirit of battle was upon him, and he longed to go forward to the fray, which proved to be the last, but not least, of his wonderful exploits.

General Burnside had been removed from command of the Federal army after the battle of Fredericksburg, and General Hooker, "Fighting Joe," as he was called, was put in his place. His army now numbered about one hundred and fifty thousand men.

General Lee's army, to the number of forty-five thousand men, lay entrenched upon the southern banks of the Rappahannock river. General Longstreet's corps was now absent in Suffolk county, so Lee had not one-third as many men as Hooker.

Hooker's plan was to divide his army into two parts. The smaller part was to cross the river near Fredericksburg and engage the Confederates in battle, while the larger part would march up the northern bank of the Rappahannock river, and, crossing over, reach the flank of Lee's army, which would thus have the foe in front and also in the rear. At the same time Hooker planned to send a large troop of cavalry to reach and destroy the railroads leading to Richmond, thus cutting General Lee off from the capital.

This was a bold plan, but one that was easily guessed by such soldiers as Lee, Jackson, and Stuart. The last named kept watch, and as soon as a movement was made, reported it to Lee. Lee at once fell back to Chancellorsville, but not until the main army under General Hooker himself had reached "The Wilderness" beyond Chancellorsville, and thrown up strong earthworks. The left wing of Hooker's army, under General Sedgwick, crossed the river below Fredericksburg on the 29th of April, and was at once met by Jackson, who was ever watchful. Sedgwick, however, did not intend to fight, but merely to keep General Lee at Fredericksburg while Hooker was gaining the point on Lee's flank. General Lee promptly guessed the plan, and ordered General Jackson to leave only one division in front of Sedgwick, to proceed at once in search of Hooker, and to attack and repulse him. This order reached Jackson about eight P. M., and by midnight his troops were on the march. Early the next day they reached the battle-field, where the troops of General Anderson were already engaged with the enemy.

Lee, Jackson, and Stuart at the battle of Fredericksburg.

Jackson halted his column, and sending four brigades to the support of Anderson, drew up the remainder of the corps in line of battle upon a ridge near by. The battle raged fiercely all day, and when night came, the Confederates had reached Hooker's first line of entrenchments, in the midst of the dense forest.

Meanwhile General Lee had come up with the remainder of the army, and a sharp fight had taken place in front of Hooker's right wing. Night put an end to the contest, when, weary and worn, both armies lay down to rest upon the battle-field.

When Lee and Jackson met that night they were joined by General Stuart, who told them that, though General Hooker had strongly fortified his position upon the east, south, and southwest, upon the north and west he had left it open. Jackson's quick mind at once planned to attack Hooker in the rear, just as Hooker had planned to attack Lee.

To the northwest, there were no earthworks, and if Jackson could surprise the Federals he would be almost sure of victory. Stuart was there with his gallant horsemen to cover this movement, and the forests were so dense that Jackson was sure of leading his men silently to the rear of Hooker.

General Lee listened to his arguments, and finally gave consent for his great lieutenant to make the trial. He (General Lee) would remain with two divisions in front to engage Hooker, while Jackson would march around and strike him in the rear.

By the aid of his chaplain, Rev. Mr. Lacy, who knew that country well, General Jackson found a road which would lead him to the rear of Hooker's army. By sunrise he was in the saddle at the head of his column.

General Stuart was there to cover his line of march, and his troops, knowing at once that their General was making one of his famous flank movements, went forward at a rapid pace. We are told by Dr. McGuire, who was with Jackson, that on the march they were met by General Fitz. Lee, who told Jackson that he would show him the whole of Hooker's army if he would go to the top of a hill near by. They went together, and Jackson carefully viewed through his glasses the Federal command. He was so wrapped up in his plans that on his return he forgot to salute or thank Fitz. Lee, but hurried on to the column, where he ordered one of his aides to go forward and tell General Rodes to cross the plank road and go straight on to the turnpike, and another aide to go to the rear of the column and see that it was kept closed up, and all along the line he kept saying, "Press on, press right on." The fiercest energy seemed to possess him. When he arrived at the plank road he sent this, his last, message to Lee: "The enemy has made a stand at Chancellorsville. I hope as soon as practicable to attack. I trust that an ever kind Providence will bless us with success." At three P. M., having marched fifteen miles, he had reached the old turnpike, and was exactly on the opposite side of the enemy to that held by General Lee.

He had left the Stonewall Brigade, under General Paxton, on the plank road, with orders to block the way to Germanna ford. He found the outposts held by Stuart's vigilant troopers, who had guarded well his advance. As soon as possible he formed his army in three lines—the division of Rodes in front, that of Colston next, and A. P. Hill's in the rear. Between five and six P. M. the word was given, and the lines marched forward into the forest.

The thickets were so dense that many of the soldiers had the clothes torn from their backs, but on they went, sometimes creeping to get through the thick undergrowth. After a march of two miles they came suddenly upon the right wing of Hooker's army. The men were scattered about, cooking and eating their suppers, wholly unconscious of the approach of the dreaded Jackson. With a wild yell, the Confederates dashed forward and drove the enemy pell-mell through the forests for three miles. Jackson's only order was "Press forward," and onward rushed his devoted men after the terrified fugitives.

At eight o'clock the line of Rodes was within a mile of Chancellorsville, still in the forest, when General Jackson ordered the fresh troops of A. P. Hill to advance to the front to relieve those of Rodes, who were worn out with marching and fighting.

He knew that Hooker would send forward other troops, so he went to the front himself to get his men in order. As he rode along the line he would say, "Men, get into line! Get into line!" Turning to Colonel Cobb, he sent him to tell General Rodes to take possession of a barricade in front, and then rode away towards the turnpike.

But before the broken ranks of Rodes could gain the barricade Hooker sent forward a large body of fresh troops, and the battle was renewed all along the line.

It was now ten o'clock, and the pale moon sent her silvery rays down into the heart of the dismal Wilderness, whose echoes awoke to the sound of tramping feet, the rattle of musketry, and the groans of the dying. Through moonlight and shadow, with these sounds ringing in his ears, Jackson rode forward to his death.

After riding up the turnpike a short distance, he found the enemy advancing. Turning, he rode back rapidly towards his own line. The Southern men lying hid in the thickets, thinking that Jackson and his staff were a squad of Northern cavalry, opened a rapid fire upon them. So deadly was their aim that nearly every horse in the party was killed. Two officers were killed, others hurt, and General Jackson himself was wounded three times. His left arm was broken just below the shoulder joint, and was also wounded lower down. A third ball had entered the palm of his right hand and broken two bones.

His left hand, so cruelly hurt, dropped by his side, and his horse, no longer controlled by the reins, ran back towards the enemy.

As the horse galloped between two trees, he passed beneath a low bough, which struck his rider in the face, tore off his cap, and threw him violently back in the saddle. He did not fall, however, but grasped the reins with his bleeding right hand, and turned him back into the road. There, the General found the greatest confusion. Horses, mad with pain and fright, were running in every direction, and in the road lay the wounded and dying.

Where General Jackson fell.

Captain Wilbourne, one of Jackson's aides, now seized the reins and stopped his horse. Seeing that the General was badly hurt, he lifted him from the saddle, almost fainting from the loss of blood. He was then laid down by the side of the road, his head resting upon Captain Wilbourne's breast, while a messenger went to summon Dr. McGuire, his chief surgeon. Soon General Hill came up, and, pulling off the General's gauntlets, found that his left arm was broken.

As the enemy were not far off, his arm was quickly bandaged with a handkerchief, and he attempted to walk. But after they had gone a few steps a litter was brought, and the General was placed upon it.

The litter was hardly in motion when the fire from the guns of the enemy became terrible. Many men were struck down by it, among whom were General Hill and one of the bearers of the litter.

The litter was placed upon the ground, and the officers lay down by it to escape death.

After awhile the fire changed, and Jackson rose to his feet and walked slowly on, leaning upon two members of his staff. General Pender, coming up, saw by the moonlight that General Jackson was badly hurt. "Ah! General," said he, "I am sorry to see that you have been wounded. The lines here are so much broken that I fear we will have to fall back."

General Pender.

Though almost fainting, Jackson raised his head, and said: "You must hold your ground, General Pender! You must hold your ground!" This was the last order of Jackson on the field.

The General, being very faint, was again placed on the litter, and the whole party moved through the forest towards the hospital at Wilderness Run.

As they were going slowly through the undergrowth, one of the men caught his foot in a grapevine and fell, letting the litter fall to the ground.

General Jackson's last order on the field: "You must hold your ground, General Pender! You must hold your ground!"

Jackson fell upon his wounded shoulder, and for the first time groaned most piteously. With great difficulty they made their way until they came to a place in the road where an ambulance was waiting. The General was placed in it, and was soon met by his surgeon, Dr. McGuire, who, having sprung into the ambulance, found the General almost pulseless.

Some spirits was given him, which revived him, and ere long he was laid tenderly in a camp bed at the hospital. Here he fell into a deep sleep. About midnight he was awakened, and told by Dr. McGuire that it was thought best to amputate his arm.

"Do what you think best, Doctor," was the calm reply.

The arm was amputated, and the ball taken out of his right hand by the skillful surgeon, and he again fell into a quiet sleep, which lasted until nine o'clock on Sunday morning.

General Hill being wounded, General Stuart was placed in command of Jackson's corps. He now determined to wait until morning to attack the strong works of Hooker, which were again in front of the Confederates.

Gen. J. E. B. Stuart.

The next morning Stuart thundered on the west, and Lee on the east and south. When the Stonewall Brigade went forward, they shouted, "Charge, and remember Jackson!" "But even as they moved from their position," says Dr. Dabney, "their General, Paxton, the friend and former adjutant of Jackson, was killed where he stood. But his men rushed forward, and, without other leader than the *name* which formed their battle-cry, swept everything before them." At ten A. M., May 3d, Chancellorsville was taken by Lee, and the Federals took refuge behind new barricades nearer to the river.

In the meantime, General Sedgwick, who had been left at Fredericksburg by General Hooker, attacked General Early, and captured a part of his command. General Lee, having Hooker in check, sent help to Early, and on Wednesday, came up himself and drove General Sedgwick back across the river, where Hooker had already retreated on Tuesday night, May 5th.

General Jubal A. Early.

When General Jackson awoke on Sunday morning, May 3d, he asked one of his aids to go to Richmond for his wife. He had sent her to that city when the Federals had begun to move across the river. His mind was clear and he stated that if he had had one more hour of daylight, he would have cut off the enemy from the United States ford, and they would have been obliged either to fight their way out or to surrender.

It was now thought best to take him to a more quiet place; so on Monday he was moved to Mr. Chandler's near Guinea's Depot, where every care was taken to make him comfortable. He seemed to take much interest in hearing of the battle on Sunday, and said of the Stonewall Brigade, "They are a noble body of men. The men who live through this war will be proud to say, 'I was one of the Stonewall Brigade.'"

He then went on to say that the name of Stonewall belonged to the men of the Brigade alone, as they had earned it by their steadfast conduct at First Manassas. He spoke also of General Rodes, and said that on account of gallant conduct, he deserved to be advanced to the rank of major-general.

The death of General Paxton gave him great distress, but he grew calmer when told of the glorious exploits of his old brigade.

General R. E. Rodes.

He was much pleased at this noble letter from General Lee:

"*General*:

I have just received your note, informing me that you were wounded. I cannot express my regret at the occurrence. Could I have directed events, I should have chosen, for the good of the country, to have been disabled in your stead.

I congratulate you upon the victory which is due to your skill and energy.

Most truly yours, (Signed) R. E. LEE, *General*."

His mind seemed ever dwelling on religious subjects, and he was entirely submissive to the will of God.

On Wednesday, his wounds were doing so well that it was thought possible to take him by railroad to Richmond. On that night, however, while Dr. McGuire was absent from him for awhile, he was taken with a severe pain in his side, which was in fact due to pneumonia, which had now set in.

From that time he grew weaker, and at last it was seen that he could live only a few hours.

Mrs. Jackson arrived on Thursday, and to her he said, "I know you would gladly give your life for me, but I am perfectly resigned." When his weeping wife at last told him that death was near, he whispered, "Very good, very good, it is all right." He then sent messages to many friends, and desired to be buried in Lexington, in the Valley of Virginia.

Julia Jackson at the age of four years.

His little girl was now brought in to receive his last farewell.

Upon seeing her, his face lit up with a bright smile, and he murmured, "Little darling!" He tried to caress her with his poor maimed hand—she smiling in her delight at seeing him again. Thus, she remained by his side upon the bed until it was seen that he was growing very weak.

Then his mind began to wander, and as if again upon the battle-field, he cried out: "Order A. P. Hill to prepare for action!" "Pass the infantry to the front!" "Tell Major Hawks to send forward provisions for the men!" Then his vision changed, and he murmured, "Let us cross over the river, and rest under the shade of the trees."

"The moment had indeed come," says Cooke, "when the great leader was to pass over the dark river which separates two worlds, and rest under the shade of the Tree of Life. From this time, he continued to sink, and at fifteen minutes past three in the afternoon, on Sunday, the 10th of May, he peacefully expired."

Pontoon', a bridge built on boats.

Furlough (fûr'lo), a short leave of absence.

Chăp'lain, a clergyman of the army or navy.

Rātions (or răsh-uns), a certain quantity of food and drink.

Vig'i lant, watchful.

Barricade', a hastily-made fortification.

Tell about—

The battle of Fredericksburg.

Jackson's life at Moss Neck.

Jackson's march around Hooker.

His death.

CHAPTER X.
Upon the Roll of Fame.

Upon hearing the news of Jackson's death, the grief of the South was equalled only by the wish to do him honor.

President Davis sent a special train to bear his remains to Richmond. He also sent, as the gift of the country, the beautiful new flag of the Confederate Congress to be his winding sheet.

Jefferson Davis

When the train reached Richmond, it was met by a vast concourse of weeping people. On Wednesday, the coffin, preceded by military, was borne from the Governor's Mansion to the Capitol through the main streets of the city. The hearse was drawn by four white horses and followed by eight generals as pallbearers. Then came his horse, caparisoned for battle, and led by his body-servant; then followed his staff, the President, the Governor of Virginia, the city authorities, and a vast number of sorrowing people.

"Fancy," or "Little Sorrel." General T. J. Jackson's War-Horse, 30 Years Old.

As the procession moved along, cannon were fired and bells tolled. At last the Capitol was reached and the body was borne, amid the tears of the multitude, into the building where it lay in state all day. Twenty thousand persons are said to have passed in front of the body to gaze for the last time upon their mighty chief.

It is said that President Davis stood long, gazing at the quiet face, and then in silence left the house.

Old soldiers pressed around the bier with tears streaming down their bronzed faces, while one stooped and kissed the cold lips of his beloved commander.

The next day the remains were borne, attended by a guard of honor, to Lexington, where they were received by General Smith, the corps of cadets, the professors, and many sorrowing citizens. They were borne to the barracks of the Military Institute and placed in the old class-room of the dead general. Every half hour, the cadet battery pealed forth a fitting requiem to the great teacher of artillery tactics. Then "escorted by infantry, cavalry, and artillery, under command of Col. Shipp, and borne to the grave upon a caisson of the cadet battery," he was laid to rest beside the graves of his first wife and child in the beautiful cemetery of Lexington.

The "right hand" of Lee was thus taken away just as the heaviest stroke had fallen upon the enemy. General Lee, the army, the whole South mourned for their fallen hero. There were other generals as brave and true as Jackson, but none who possessed his keen insight into the movements of the enemy, his celerity of action, and the wonderful certainty of victory which made him the idol of his own soldiers and the dread of the foe.

But the renown of Jackson is not confined to the limits of his own land. It has crossed the ocean, and now the plans of his battles in the Valley of the Shenandoah and of Second Manassas and of Chancellorsville are studied by military men, and used by them as models of strategy and tactics. All English-speaking people are justly proud that the greatest military genius of the age belongs to them.

Jackson's Statue in Capitol Square, Richmond, Va.

Not long after the end of the war, his admirers and friends in England presented to the State of Virginia a statue of Jackson in bronze. It was placed in the Capitol Square in Richmond not far from the statue of Washington and the great Virginians of his time.

In the spring of 1891, a beautiful and imposing statue of our hero was erected in Lexington, Virginia, by his old soldiers and friends throughout the South. On July 21st of that year, it was unveiled in the presence of a vast multitude of people.

The anniversary of the First Manassas, when Jackson, in a "baptism of fire," received the new name of "Stonewall," and flashed like a meteor upon the wondering world, was thought a fitting day on which to display to his countrymen his figure in enduring bronze.

For days and nights, the trains bore into the historic town crowds of soldiers and visitors from all parts of the country. Beautiful arches and mottoes graced the buildings and highways, and the whole was crowned by perfect weather.

At 12 o'clock, the great parade moved from the Virginia Military Institute. General James A. Walker, the only commander of the Stonewall Brigade then living, was chief marshal of the day.

As the procession moved on, band after band of Confederates were seen—battle-scarred veterans in the old Confederate grey, military companies in bright uniforms, famous generals with bronzed faces and grizzled hair, the chaplains of the Confederacy, and visiting camps of veterans from other States.

Following these came the officers of the Virginia Military Institute and Washington and Lee University. Finally came a large concourse of citizens and carriages. Among those in the carriages were General Jubal A. Early, the orator of the day, and his host, General Custis Lee; the sculptor of the statue, Edward V. Valentine; Mrs. General T. J. Jackson and her son-in-law, Mr. Christian, and his children, Julia and Thomas Jackson Christian.

At last, the grand-stand in the University grounds was reached. After prayer and the reading of three Confederate war poems, "Stonewall Jackson's Way," "Slain in Battle," and "Over the River," General Early, clad in Confederate grey, made the address, which gave a simple account of the great battles fought by Jackson. He was greeted with hearty cheers, and tears rolled down the checks of many veterans as they again in memory fought and marched with the immortal Jackson.

At the end of the speech the procession again formed and marched to the cemetery where stood the monument.

At the given signal, Mrs. Jackson and her two grandchildren, Julia Jackson Christian, aged five years, and Thomas Jackson Christian, aged three years, mounted the steps of the platform. A single gun sounded, and the two children with united hands pulled the cord and let the veil fall, revealing to admiring thousands the face and form of Jackson.

Cheers and shouts rent the air, while the Rockbridge Artillery fired a salute of fifteen guns from the cannon which they had used at Manassas.

The statue, clad in the uniform of a major-general, stands with the left hand grasping a sheathed sword, upon which the weight of the body seems to rest. The right hand rests upon the thigh and holds a pair of field glasses, which it would seem that the General has just been using.

The figure is eight feet high and stands upon a granite pedestal ten feet tall. Upon the stone are carved only the words, "Jackson, 1824-1863," and "Stonewall."

Under the monument, in a vault, rest the remains of the dead soldier and his daughters, Mrs. Christian, and Mary Graham who died in infancy.

Jackson Statue at Lexington.

The veterans lingered long about their beloved hero. Many times had they followed him on the weary march and through the smoke of battle, and now it seemed as if he were with them again to lead them on to victory.

At last, saluting, they marched in silence away, carrying his image in their memories and the love of him in their hearts.

Perhaps it will interest my readers to have a pen and ink portrait of Mrs. Jackson at that time, as given by a leading journalist of the day. "Mrs. Jackson sat just behind the famous generals. She wore a handsome costume of black silk trimmed with crepe, black gloves, and a crepe bonnet. Her face is a most attractive one. Her black hair, still unmixed with grey, was brushed in graceful waves across her forehead. Her eyes, large and dark, sparkled and filled with tears, as veteran after veteran pressed forward to grasp her hand."

Not long before, her daughter, Mrs. Christian, the baby Julia whom Jackson had loved so well, had died, leaving two children, Julia and Thomas. These children are the only descendants of our beloved General. At this writing, in the year of our Lord 1898, Mrs. Jackson is still living, and to her the hearts of Southern people turn in fond affection, because she was the best beloved of their mighty chief.

But not enough had been done to honor our hero. In 1896, a noble building called the "Jackson Memorial Hall" was completed at the Virginia Military Institute, and dedicated with fitting ceremony to the memory of Jackson. In these halls and beneath the shadow of this building, the cadets of the South for many long years will be trained for war. How fit the place! Near by rest Lee and Stonewall Jackson—mighty soldiers, and Christian warriors!

Jackson Memorial Hall, Virginia Military Institute.

There the sweeping winds proclaim our heroes' fame, and nightly the glittering stars chant in heavenly chorus: "They shine, they shine with our brightness."

Cā-is-son, a chest for ammunition.

Capăr'isoned, dressed pompously.

Tăc'tics, the science and art of placing forces for battle.

Rē'quiem, a hymn sung for the dead.

Vĕte'ran, one who has grown old in service.

Pĕd'-es-tal, the base of a column or statue.

Write in your own words—

A description of the reception of General Jackson's body in Richmond.

A description of his monument in Lexington, Virginia.

CPSIA information can be obtained
at www.ICGtesting.com
Printed in the USA
LVHW041013020323
740706LV00008B/984

9 789356 904156